Presented To:

From:

Date:

JOURNEY

—— OF A ——

WORLD
CHANGER

DESTINY IMAGE BOOKS BY BANNING LIEBSCHER

Jesus Culture

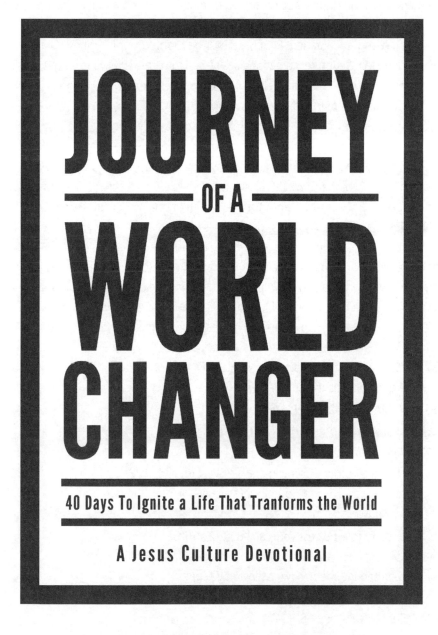

JOURNEY
OF A
WORLD
CHANGER

40 Days To Ignite a Life That Tranforms the World

A Jesus Culture Devotional

BANNING LIEBSHER

DESTINY IMAGE® PUBLISHERS, INC.

P.O. Box 310, Shippensburg, PA 17257-0310

"Promoting Inspired Lives."

This book and all other Destiny Image, Revival Press, MercyPlace, Fresh Bread, Destiny Image Fiction, and Treasure House books are available at Christian bookstores and distributors worldwide.

For a U.S. bookstore nearest you, call 1-800-722-6774.

For more information on foreign distributors, call 717-532-3040.

Reach us on the Internet: www.destinyimage.com.

ISBN 13 TP: 978-0-7684-0293-3

ISBN 13 Ebook: 978-0-7684-8796-1

For Worldwide Distribution, Printed in the U.S.A.

5 6 7 8 / 16 15 14

DEDICATION

To my three world changers, Ellianna, Raya, and Lake.
I love being on this journey with you.
You make my heart proud.

ACKNOWLEDGEMENTS

This book could never happened without some amazing people investing their time, energy, and support into it.

Dave Harvey, thank you for taking what was on my heart and helping me take a generation deeper. A.J. Butel, thank you once again for making me look smarter than I am. Pam Spinosi, you consistently raise the bar of excellence in my life. To the team that helped me get this concept together—Michael, Becky, Zack, Tom, Dana, Charles, your insight and wisdom was invaluable. To all those who have a testimony in this book, thank you for letting us share your story.

ENDORSEMENTS

As I have lived a life dedicated to being a world changer, I have realized that much of what I am called to do is based on my willingness to just position myself. It's not about who's great, it's about who is willing to be available for a greater call.

I am a huge fan of Banning's heart and message for this generation, and I know you will greatly benefit from this book! He gives amazing insight into becoming the world changer you were born to be. Take your place. History is waiting for you.

ALYSSA BARLOW
Christian Recording Artist

Banning is one of the most anointed, gifted, and dedicated leaders in our generation. He continually stirs us with a "follow me as I follow Christ" lifestyle, and thousands are doing just that. Anything Banning is a part of is worth your time and effort. It hasn't come without a hidden life in Christ and a dedication few men possess. This book will equip you with earthly tools and heavenly realities to live a life of passionate pursuit and set your life spinning into spiritual awakening.

HAVILAH CUNNINGTON
Writer, speaker, teaching pastor
www.havilahcunnington.com

I highly recommend *Journey of a World Changer*. I firmly believe this journal will ignite your faith and evoke a hunger to be used mightily by God. Banning illustrates essential truths that are sure to accelerate you in your journey.

BRANDON SMITH
Student Leader, Campus Awakening, UC Berkeley
Twitter:@followsmitty

Ditch mediocrity. Hear God. Overcome lust. Make history! Two thousand years ago, Jesus transformed ordinary men into extraordinary world changers, and He's still doing it today. In this journal, Banning Liebscher takes you by the hand and leads you in opportunity after opportunity to encounter Jesus so that you too can change the world! Students and youth pastors everywhere must get their hands on this book!

DAVID PERKINS
DesperationOnline.com

It's very rare to find a leader as gifted and humble as Banning Liebscher. What I love most about Banning and this book is that he is able to take the supernatural and make it practical to a generation that desires the supernatural and the practical. The journey of a world changer is exactly what Banning's life has been. I can't think of anyone more qualified to write this book. Our generation needs to read, then apply…and go on the journey of a world changer.

CHAD VEACH
United Generation Pastor, Foursquare Church in Washington

In *Journey of a World Changer,* Banning calls this generation from mediocrity to royalty. He invites people across the world who feel trapped in fear and regret to step out and take the Kingdom—and their lives—by force. He challenges us to make a decision; to either ignore the reality of why we're created, or to abandon everything and take up the authority God has gifted us with since before time began. With absolute humility and uncommon depth, Banning relentlessly speaks life and love over this generation and brings out the warrior in every believer. Get it, read it, live it, and watch everything change.

SHANE ROGERS
Pastor, Generation United, a youth ministry of
The Church of Living Water, Olympia, Washington
Director, Repossess, a city-wide youth movement

CONTENTS

HOW TO USE THIS BOOK

The aim of *Journey of a World Changer* is to help you to practically walk out some of the main concepts from my book *Jesus Culture—Living A Life That Transforms the World*. I really want to encourage you to take time to spend with the Lord as you go through it. I know that as you walk through this book with Him, that He will radically transform both you and your world!

You can use this book as a personal journey or you can do it with 3-4 friends over the 40 days (*see back of the book for "How to use this book with friends") At the beginning of each day is a quote from my book *Jesus Culture* which will help you to see where each days concept 'ties' into the main book.

There are five sections in this 40-day journey that correspond directly to my book:

- ## SECTION 1—THE NEW BREED
  - Reflection day

- ## SECTION 2—UNDER COVERING
  - Reflection day

- ## SECTION 3—THE BURNING ONES
  - Reflection day

- ## SECTION 4—THOSE WHO PRAY
  - Reflection day

- ## SECTION 5—HEALING REVIVALISTS
  - Reflection day

At the end of each section is a Reflection day. This day will have a different format in order to help you to pause and reflect on what God has been teaching and doing in your life over the previous section. These days are really important to help you 'solidify' and 'establish' what God is doing in your life.

HOW EACH DAY IS STRUCTURED

There are five basic components to each daily journey—Quote, Testimony of a World Changer, Discipleship, Prayer, Activation & Further Reading.

🌍 QUOTE

As mentioned above, this inspiring quote will help you see how the day's concept ties into the main book. This will also help you to dive deeper into the concept if you want to read more from the original book.

💬 TESTIMONY OF A WORLD CHANGER

These are some of the best testimonies from around the world of real people, from all ages, and spheres of life - who are changing their world. Be encouraged and use these as resources to enlarge your vision to what God can do through your life each day!

👥 DISCIPLESHIP:

The discipleship component of each day will focus on one main concept through a short 'meaty' teaching and some questions. The aim is for you to focus on one thing for that day and apply that concept to your life over the coming 24hrs. Take time to answer the questions and make sure you answer truthfully from your heart. Its when we bring things into the light that God can bring transformation.

 PRAYER:

Each day I want you to be mobilized into encountering God through praying scripture! Each day there will be three scriptures for you to pray—one focused on God and two focused on you and your world. You can praise and worship God from these verses, declare them over your life and pray them into your world. Be creative and follow the leading of the Holy Spirit as you release heaven into earth.

ACTIVATION:

To wrap up each day, I have included one challenge, which will help you to practice that concept in your world each day. I believe that these challenges will cause you to do things that you have never imagined were possible, and will help you to step into your true identity as a son or daughter of God. Make sure you record the testimonies of what God does through you and reflect on what He is teaching you about Himself and yourself each day!

FURTHER READING

Finally at the end of the day will also be some further reading from the Bible if you want to explore concept with God even more.

Remember, God is an adventurous God and He is not confined to the outline of the book. So make sure you are attentive to His voice throughout and follow where He leads you to go. Are you ready to see your world transformed? Lets go!

INTRODUCTION

I didn't realize at the time, but it was a defining moment in my life. I was saved when I was four years old, but there at the front of the church, as I knelt before the altar at the age of 17, I felt the Lord calling me to a journey of complete abandonment. It was in that moment I decided to give 100 percent of my life to serving Jesus. And in an instant, everything changed.

I went home that night knowing what God had called me to. My heart had been awakened to Jesus in a fresh way, and the result was an awareness and passion for His cause in the earth. I never knew I was a leader until then. I hadn't understood my life was fashioned to change the course of world history. But something catalytic began to stir deep within, and I embarked on the journey I am still experiencing today.

I wrote *Jesus Culture* because the Lord spoke clearly to me about your life. He showed me there was a new breed of revivalist emerging in the earth today because God's heart was burning for campuses, cities, and nations. You are part of that new breed. I believe lives will be saved, communities restored, and nations transformed because you have been commissioned to change the world.

The Journey of a World Changer is designed to ignite within you a devotion to dive deeper and embrace more fully and effectively the assignment to be used by God to make a difference. You were created to affect the course of world history. Everything else is boring!

On this 40-day journey of discovery and empowerment, you will find God has called you to be a leader who impacts the world.

Will you take this journey with me? Will you wholeheartedly abandon yourself to Jesus and His desire in the earth? Will you choose surrender—and become a world changer?

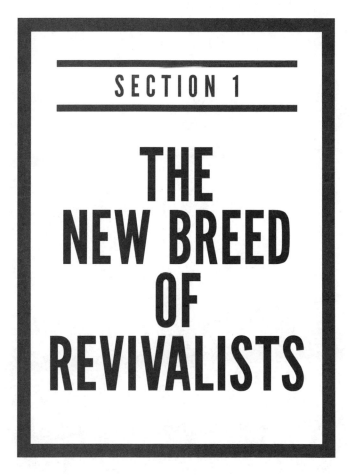

SECTION 1

THE
NEW BREED
OF
REVIVALISTS

DAY 1
YOU ARE A WORLD CHANGER!

YOU HAVE BEEN STRATEGICALLY PLACED BY
GOD TO TRANSFORM YOUR WORLD.

God searched throughout the corridors of eternity and decided to strategically place you in this exact dispensation of time…. God has chosen to put you right here, right now for the greatest outpouring the world has ever seen. (Liebscher 2009, 28)[1]

TESTIMONY OF A WORLD CHANGER

A group of Hindu women sat on the ground in a crowded marketplace. One was suffering from a painful eye disease and was going blind. Her friend, lying beside her on a mat, was unable to walk. They were listening intently to a small solar audio Bible.

When they heard the dramatized voice of blind Bartimaeus crying out to Jesus, the blind woman began calling out as well. Suddenly, she realized that her eyes were healed.

When the lame woman heard the story of Jesus instructing the lame man, "Take up your bed and walk," she immediately stood and picked up her mat.

There was no missionary present, but these Hindu women had encountered Jesus and were part of a church-planting revolution:

Researchers showed the Jesus film in 500 villages in India. Before departing, they entrusted an audio Bible to a responsible villager. When the researchers returned six months later, they found over 17,000 people meeting regularly to listen to God's Word.

It's been 2,000 years since Jesus sent us to every nation, yet 2,000 languages still have not one verse of Scripture. Pray that God will send out a mighty army of harvesters. What is your part?

STEPHANIE, Missionary

 ## DISCIPLESHIP

You are a world changer and have been strategically placed! Whenever God wants to reveal Himself in a region to save the lost and transform society through His presence and power, He anoints and commissions individuals we call *world changers*. World changers are fearless and powerful. They know they are citizens of Heaven whose passion is to make a difference in the earth. In Acts 17 it says:

> *From one man He made all the people of the world. Now they live all over the earth. He decided exactly when they should live. And he decided exactly where they should live* (Acts 17:26 NIRV).

God's plan has been and continues to be to plant world changers all across the planet, strategically positioned to make a difference and bring Heaven to earth.

How does it make you feel to know God has set you in the exact place He wants you, to bring Heaven to earth?

_____

_____

_____

Esther was a young woman who realized God had sent her to be a world changer. She also understood He had deliberately placed her in the royal palace to make a difference. Esther knew she wasn't alive just to

WHAT IF...*you truly began to believe and live like you were created, positioned, and endorsed by God to change your world?*

enjoy the royal palace and all the pleasures and benefits it would bring; rather, she grasped the revelation that she was intentionally placed there, "for such a time as this." When a plot was revealed to eradicate the people of God, Esther arose in her identity and the influence God had given her to save the Jews from complete annihilation. Genocide was thwarted! But it took the courage and wisdom of a world changer. Esther's obedience and sacrifice affected the lives of millions.

WHAT IF...like Esther, you realized how significant and special you are?

Esther had to listen to and believe Mordecai's encouragement of how significant she was. Ask God to tell you what strengths He has placed in you. Write down at least three and thankfully declare these over your life.

_____

_____

What makes you come alive? What causes your heart to burn? Ask the Lord how your life can bring His Kingdom into this area/activity/issue.

_____

_____

YOU ARE CALLED...to arise in courage and responsibility for the people within your sphere of influence.

Ask God to show you who is in your sphere of influence. Which group of people in the world does your heart go out to?

_____

_____

How does it make you feel to know that, just like Esther, God has called you to be a world changer who influences many?

_____

_____

PRAYER

Get alone with God. Welcome the Holy Spirit and thank Him for all the good things in your life.

Use the Scripture below to worship God and declare how great He is:

> And it shall come to pass in the last days, says God, That I will pour out of My Spirit on all flesh (Acts 2:17).

Jesus, You are the God who will pour Your Spirit on all flesh! Spend some time praying these Scriptures over your life:

> From one man he made all the people of the world. Now they live all over the earth. He decided exactly when they should live. And he decided exactly where they should live. God did this so that people would seek him. Then perhaps they would reach out for him and find him. They would find him even though he is not far from any of us (Acts 17:26-27 NIRV).

Jesus, You have decided exactly where I should live.

> …Yet who knows whether you have come to the kingdom for such a time as this? (Esther 4:14)

Jesus, You have led me into the Kingdom for such a time as this.

ACTIVATION

Esther was also a woman of prayer. Once she realized who she was and the immensity of what God was calling her to, she fasted and prayed.

Spend time praying for those who are in your sphere of influence. Make a list of three people you could begin to pray for. Ask God for specific things He wants you to pray for them.

> **WHAT IF…***you humbly and passionately interceded on behalf of those you have been entrusted with?*

_____

_____

Ask Him what He wants you to do to bless them today. This could be a word of encouragement or an opportunity to bless. Write down some ideas and then have fun demonstrating His heart.

_____

_____

TODAY IS THE DAY WHEN YOU BEGIN TO WALK LIKE YOU HAVE BEEN STRATEGICALLY PLACED BY GOD TO TRANSFORM YOUR WORLD!

FURTHER REFLECTION

Read Esther 4:11-17. Ask God what He wants you to capture from the story. Meditate on the things He shows you and begin to pray for these areas to be made manifest in and through your life.

NOTE

1. Banning Liebscher, *Jesus Culture: Living a Life That Transforms the World* (Shippensburg, PA: Destiny Image, 2009).

EARTH LIKE HEAVEN

YOU HAVE BEEN AUTHORIZED AND EMPOWERED TO MAKE YOUR WORLD LIKE HEAVEN.

When God finds someone with the courage to preach, pray, and live a life before Him of holiness and compassion, He can literally change the face of a nation. (Winkie Pratney, Revival, quoted in Lieb-scher, 143)

💬 TESTIMONY OF A WORLD CHANGER

All my life I have been saved. Although I was raised in the church by an amazing family who loved me, I lived life continuously not knowing who I was. There was always a genuine love for God inside me and a hunger for more. I never quite understood how to go after Him, so I didn't make the best of choices. I always felt there was something different about me— something I didn't see in the kids around me.

At the age of 12, I went to my first Jesus Culture Conference in Redding, California! At this conference my eyes were open to realize God is not just somebody you talk about, but He is a personal Being who loves me and desires to impact the places around me, through me. I had a radical en-counter with God and heard Him say, "Dominic, you're a part of this new breed of revivalists that is going to change the world." I responded to the call, abandoning myself to Him. Ever since that time, I know I'm a world changer and God has called me for such a time as this.

DOMINIC, high school student, age 16

👥 DISCIPLESHIP

God's original calling was for every person to be a world changer. In the beginning He placed humankind in a garden of paradise and commissioned them with a "world-changing" mandate: *"Be fruitful and multiply; fill the earth and subdue it; have dominion…"* (Gen. 1:28).

From this commission we can conclude that inside the garden everything was amazing, but outside Eden there were things needing to be brought into alignment and reconnection to God. The Lord's original plan for humankind was not to be passive but to be initiators in restoring and healing every area on the planet.

When Jesus came onto the scene thousands of years later, He reinstated us to this original assignment of being a world changer. In Matthew 6:10, He authorized us to pray, *"Your kingdom come. Your will be done, on earth as it is in heaven."*

Jesus gave us authority to release the resources of Heaven into every area of our world that was controlled by darkness. This means where there is sickness, we are given authority to release healing. Where there is poverty, we can pray and release prosperity. Into any area of lack in our world, Jesus has enabled us to speak Heaven's abundance.

WHAT COULD YOU DO…if you truly believed you were authorized and empowered by God to release Heaven's abundance into your world?

In Matthew 10:8, Jesus further empowered us as world changers. He told His disciples, *"Heal the sick, cleanse the lepers, raise the dead, cast out demons. Freely you have received, freely give."* So they went out in pairs and impacted whole cities for God. When they returned, Jesus said, *"I saw Satan fall like lightning from heaven"* (Luke 10:18).

WHAT IF…*Jesus asked us to pray "on earth as it is in Heaven" because He actually wanted to do it?*

Today, Jesus has endorsed and commissioned *you* to heal the sick, cleanse the lepers, raise the dead, and cast out demons. He has anointed you with Holy Spirit power to impact cities, turn nations to God, and see Satan fall like lightning!

Describe three negative situations that are in your world. What could Heaven's "remodeling" of these look like?

_____

_____

_____

Read Jeremiah 29:11-12. Think about how the landscape of your friends' lives would appear if they had God's plans at work in and through them. For example: "peace," "not evil," "a future," and "hope."

WHAT IF...you aligned your thoughts and prayers with the mindset of Heaven and persevered until you saw its demonstration upon the earth?

PRAYER

Get alone with God. Welcome the Holy Spirit to come and speak as you read. Spend some time thanking Him for all the good things in your life.

As you did yesterday, use this Scripture below to worship God and declare how great He is:

> *Of the increase of His government and peace there will be no end, upon the throne of David and over His kingdom, to order it and establish it with judgment and justice from that time forward, even forever. The zeal of the Lord of hosts will perform this* (Isaiah 9:7).

Jesus, You are the God of peace and justice, and Your government will not stop increasing!

Spend some time praying these Scriptures over your life:

> *In this manner, therefore, pray: Our Father in heaven, hallowed be Your name. Your kingdom come. Your will be done on earth as it is in heaven* (Matthew 6:9-10).

Jesus, You have given me authority to release Heaven to earth!

> *For* [I am] *God's masterpiece. He has created* [me] *anew in Christ Jesus, so* [I] *can do the good things he planned for* [me] *long ago* (Ephesians 2:10 NLT).

Jesus, You made me a masterpiece and have good plans for my life.

ACTIVATION

Write down the good things God has placed in your life. Begin to thank Him and pray for His Kingdom to be increased in and through you. For example: His divine health, His love, His wisdom, His peace.

Think of others who need what you have and pray that these blessings from Heaven would fill their lives, too.

TODAY, USE YOUR AUTHORITY AND POWER TO MAKE YOUR WORLD LIKE HEAVEN!

FURTHER REFLECTION

Read Matthew 6:9-10. Ask the Lord to show what He is teaching you in these verses.

DAY 3
TUNING IN

YOU WERE CREATED TO HEAR GOD'S VOICE.

God is always talking to us, and we must incline our ear to hear His voice. (Liebscher, 35)

💬 TESTIMONY OF A WORLD CHANGER

My friend seemed to be having a challenging time trying to figure out the next step in his journey, and was at a conference where a few friends and I were working at a booth. I wanted to encourage him, and when I asked if we could all pray for him, God gave me a really clear picture of a squadron of helicopters flying over a jungle. I sensed my friend was leading this team. After I shared what I saw, he stared at me, baffled; "How did you know?"

"Know what?" I asked.

"I've been considering applying to helicopter flight school with the Air Force in Portland to become a squadron leader!"

God knows our hearts!

LEIGH, BSSM Student, age 31

 **DISCIPLESHIP**

Today's world changers are recognizing that God is communicating to them more than they ever imagined. King David had a revelation of how much God was speaking when he said:

> **WHAT IF...**_hearing God's voice is easier than you think?_

> *How precious also are Your thoughts to me, O God! How great is the sum of them! If I should count them, they would be more in number than the sand...* (Psalms 139:17-18).

One of the ways world changers hear the Lord is in their minds. One way to be sure it is Him speaking is by remaining accountable to the message of the written Word of God. The Scriptures are the basis for our life, and every thought God uses to speak to us must be congruent with the Bible.

DID YOU KNOW...God is transmitting encouraging, creative, and world-changing thoughts—even more than you could have ever hoped or imagined?

The Bible says we can know these thoughts of God and be instructed by them, because, "we have the mind of Christ" (1 Cor. 2:16).

By faith, we hear God speaking in our "redeemed" or "made right with God" minds. This can come as a thought, a picture, or an impression. Jesus said:

> *Which of you, if his son asks for bread, will give him a stone? Or if he asks for a fish, will give him a snake? If you, then, though you are evil, know how to give good gifts to your children, how much more will your Father in heaven give good gifts to those who ask him!* (Matthew 7:9-11 NIV)

As world changers, if we ask God questions, we can be sure He answers. As His children, we can tap into our Father's thoughts for family, friends, workplace, and the world! We just need to learn to incline the ears of our heart to receive what He is saying. The Holy Spirit teaches us to discern the Lord's voice.

How often do you think the Lord is speaking to you in your mind? What does that usually look like to you? For example, do you receive words, pictures, or feelings?

_____

_____

What do you think would happen if you began to ask Him specific questions and then listen for His response in your mind? Ask God about a specific issue that you or someone else is facing. Ask Him for one of His thoughts about how to release Heaven into that situation.

_____

_____

WHAT IF...God is not speaking angrily toward you at all?

Have you ever felt like God's tone with you was angry and condemning? Give an example.

_____

_____

Read Philippians 4:8 and First Corinthians 14:3. How do these Scriptures reveal an understanding of how your Father in Heaven will talk to you and to others?

_____

_____

IMAGINE...living a life with a Father who only has positive, empowering, and uplifting thoughts for you.

Spend some time praying and thanking Him for speaking words of edification, exhortation, and comfort toward you.

((•)) PRAYER

Get alone with God. Welcome the Holy Spirit and thank Him for all the good things in your life.

Use this Scripture below to worship God and declare how great He is:

> *Most assuredly, I say to you, the hour is coming, and now is, when the dead will hear the voice of the Son of God; and those who hear will live* (John 5:25).

Jesus, You speak to me and Your voice causes me to live.
Spend some time praying these Scriptures over your life:

> *For "who has known the mind of the Lord that he may instruct Him?" But we have the mind of Christ* (1 Corinthians 2:16).

Jesus, You have given me Your mind and I can hear Your voice.

> *You hear, O Lord, the desire of the afflicted; you encourage them, and you listen to their cry* (Psalms 10:17 NIV).

Jesus, You encourage me when I cry out to You!

ACTIVATION

Ask God who *He* says you are. Write down the word or draw the picture. Ask Him what gifts He has placed in your life. Again, record the words or pictures.

_____

_____

Ask Him for a Scripture declaring who *you* are. Write this down and display it somewhere prominent as a reminder. Consider and absorb what He is saying.

_____

_____

WHY NOT TAKE SOME TIME TODAY TO LISTEN TO GOD'S VOICE IN YOUR MIND AND SEE WHAT HE SAYS?

FURTHER REFLECTION

Read Psalms 139:1-6,17-18. Meditate and pray about the things God shows you.

Recommended Reading: *Face to Face with God* by Bill Johnson.

UNEARTHING TREASURE

YOU WERE CREATED TO PROPHESY AND BUILD PEOPLE UP BY CALLING FORTH THEIR GOLD.

Prayer is really just us finding out what God wants to do and then going back to Him and asking Him to do that. Through prophetic revelation, the Lord draws our focus to what He is doing. (Liebscher, 160)

💬 TESTIMONY OF A WORLD CHANGER

I was with a group of friends sitting at a coffee shop asking God for pictures to draw for people down the street. When I closed my eyes, I saw the Australian outback, and a windmill with a small house beside it. Rising up from the ground was a huge wave about to dump on the house. I thought, "This is wrong! I am in America…this picture can't be right!" Reluctantly I drew it, but as I meditated on the picture, I felt like God said, "It is for a father who has a son. I want you to write down that I am about to wash joy and peace over him."

We drove down to the mall, and just happened to park right outside the Outback restaurant. It took me a minute to realize and I exclaimed, "Hey, I drew the Australian outback! We must be in the right place!" Then I saw a man with a young boy on his shoulders walking to his car. So I nervously approached him and began to describe the picture and word of encouragement. The man began to break down and cry, sharing how his wife had recently filed for divorce. We asked if we could pray with him and he said, "Yes, please!" The man was so comforted by the prophetic picture that he took it home, framed it, and put it on his wall! I bumped into the man regularly for months afterward, and he kept thanking me for that word from God because it changed his life and gave him hope!

Jaden, student, age 18

DISCIPLESHIP

Jesus' new world-changing team has been equipped with some of the most powerful weapons to destroy darkness and bring light. When the Holy Spirit came in power on Pentecost, He endowed supernatural gifts of *power* such as gifts of prophecy, words of knowledge, and healing. And He still does the same today, enabling every believer to bring Heaven to earth.

You will receive power when the Holy Spirit has come upon you, and you will be My witnesses… (Acts 1:8 ESV).

This transference of power always points to Jesus and has been operating in believers' lives since He rose from the dead, right until this present day. The use of supernatural gifts flourishes in the faith and boldness that rises from a believer's identity solidly founded on the Father's love, the indwelling fire of the Holy Spirit, and a community of radical world changers who are supporting and propelling one another forward in the Kingdom.

PROPHECY: CALLING OUT THE GOLD

One of these gifts is prophecy. Every Christian is given the supernatural ability to hear encouraging messages from the Holy Spirit and then speak them into another person's life. This is what we call "prophecy." In First Corinthians 14:1, Paul says, "Pursue love, and desire spiritual gifts, but especially that you may prophesy." As far as Paul was concerned, every world-changing Christian needs to pursue, practice, strengthen, and grow this gift called prophecy.

Paul continues, "He who prophesies speaks edification and exhortation and comfort to men" (1 Cor. 14:3). Today's world changers are not interested in using prophecy to point out people's sin or "dirt," but they are passionate about unearthing the hidden treasure in people's lives. They do this because they understand that "the kindness of God leads you to repentance" (Rom. 2:4 NASB).

IMAGINE...what your world would be like if everyone called forth the gold *(strengths, gifts, graces)* **which people carried.**

As Christians we are called the "light of the world." Light reveals the colors and beauty of others. Prophecy is about unveiling who people truly are in Christ. One of the most powerful tools of a world changer is the ability to simply ask God for a word for someone, then draw, paint, or write it down—and present it in love.

What are two things you could do to pursue and develop the spiritual gift of prophecy?

_____

_____

What would your world be like if everyone began to call out the gold in each other? How could this simple tool change people's lives?

_____

_____

CAN YOU BELIEVE...you have been given all power and authority in Jesus?

Read Matthew 16:16-20. What did the Holy Spirit show you in this story?

_____

_____

_____

_____

Who was involved in prophesying in these verses, and what kind of words did they say?

_____

_____

What was the result of Jesus' prophetic word for Peter? How did it make Peter feel? Who eventually would have been blessed as a result of this prophetic word?

_____

What encouragement could the Lord give to those in leadership around you?

> **WHAT IF...***God gave you a word for a teacher, boss, community leader, or government official?*

_____

_____

(((•))) PRAYER

Get alone with God. Welcome the Holy Spirit, and thank Him for all the good things in your life.

Use this Scripture below to worship God and declare how great He is:

And He put all things under His feet, and gave Him to be head over all things to the church (Ephesians 1:22).

Jesus, You are powerful and have given Your power to me.
Spend some time praying these Scriptures over your life:

His divine power has given to us all things that pertain to life and godliness, through the knowledge of Him who called us by glory and virtue (2 Peter 1:3).

Jesus, You have given me divine power to help me bring life to this world.

Pursue love, and desire spiritual gifts, but especially that you may prophesy (1 Corinthians 14:1).

Jesus, You have given me the ability to prophesy.

ACTIVATION

Ask God for a picture for a friend or unsaved relative in your life who is not a Christian. Draw it, and then write down the message from God for them. Make sure it is encouraging, positive, and inspiring.

_____

_____

TAKE TIME TODAY TO PROPHESY AND BUILD PEOPLE UP BY CALLING OUT THEIR GOLD.

FURTHER REFLECTION

Read Isaiah 61:1-4 as a prophecy from Jesus to you. Highlight some of the key words of what His Spirit will empower you to do in your world.

DAY 5
A FORCE UNRESTRAINED

YOUR NEW MINDSET IS "NOTHING IS IMPOSSIBLE."

This new breed is going to be unstoppable. They will be so confi-dent in who they are and so passionate about bringing Heaven to earth that nothing else will matter. They will believe that nothing is impossible, and adhere to the words of Jesus "…all things are pos-sible to him who believes" (Mark 9:23). This is an "all things are pos-sible" generation. (Liebscher, 52)

💬 TESTIMONY OF A WORLD CHANGER

I was working at the pool as a lifeguard one afternoon, when only one hour into my shift a 23-year-old man drowned. The victim's friend, who had swum him to the side of the pool, began weeping as he realized his friend was dead. The other lifeguards and I quickly checked the victim, noting there was no pulse or breathing. They swung into action, applying CPR and AED shocks to attempt to restart his heart. However, no matter how hard they tried, all their attempts failed, and the man went into spasms as his body shut down. I stood back, remembering from my train-ing that it was now impossible for this man to live—he had been dead for over six minutes! Then I suddenly snapped out of my daze and declared, "Jesus, have Your way." I began to pray for the victim in tongues. Remark-ably, after only three seconds of praying, he took a deep breath, opened his eyes, and began breathing! He had been raised from the dead! When the paramedics arrived, they took over and rushed him to hospital. I later heard from the hospital he was 100 percent healthy. He had no brain damage and was making a full recovery! The paramedics didn't believe he had been dead for seven minutes; however when they saw the AED machine records of seven minutes, they could only admit a miracle had taken place!

CALEB, lifeguard, age 17

DISCIPLESHIP

Today God is raising up a movement of world changers who have a new mindset that nothing is impossible. They have rejected the lies of the enemy (such as God does not heal or intervene in situations anymore), and they are pressing forward to see how much of God's glory can invade the earth in their lifetime.

This new breed understands their authority and acts on it. They are unstoppable. In fact, they are so convinced about who they are and so passionate about bringing Heaven to earth, that nothing else matters (Liebscher, 52).

Jesus not only established this powerful new mindset, but He gave us His power to perform miracles. When He walked with His disciples, He established the new mindset: "Heal the sick, cleanse the lepers, raise the dead, cast out demons" (Matt. 10:8).

He even told his followers, "You will say to this mountain, 'Move from here to there,' and it will move; and nothing will be impossible for you" (Matt. 17:20). Then He died and rose again, sending the Holy Spirit so we could "receive power" (Acts 1:8) to accomplish what He told us we could do.

The miraculous realm is usually outside what is ordinarily familiar, convenient, or socially acceptable. However, Christians are now beginning to move beyond their "comfort zones" in their schools and workplaces to release healing, miracles, and signs and wonders like never before.

Comfort zones are the cultural norms and attitudes that place us in passive mode. Aaron McMahon had a choice between staying in his comfort zone or praying for a colleague on a conference call. He had to get over the thought, "Dude, you're in a business conference call. This is the wrong time and place for prayer!" He had to choose to step into the new mindset of: "I know what this is going to cost me in terms of pride and comfort, but it will be worth it when she's healed!" (Liebscher, 49)

Miracles are always just a step beyond the bounds of our safe perceptions, tendencies, and boundaries. The new mindset of a world changer isn't, "Perhaps God will show up." Instead, a world changer is at rest in God's goodness and love. Today, every believer in Jesus has access to the world-changing power of the Holy Spirit, and with Him they can release healings, miracles, signs and wonders!

WHAT COULD GOD DO THROUGH YOUR LIFE...if you believed with all your heart, "God is with me, so nothing is impossible"?

Read Acts 3:1-13. What did the Holy Spirit highlight to you in this story? What do you think He wants to show you?

_____

_____

What had just recently happened in previous chapters, enabling Peter and John to be filled with boldness to release healing to the lame man?

_____

_____

What was the result of this miracle? Who was affected?

_____

_____

Begin to declare the things you want to see happen as you step out in faith.

_____

_____

((•)) PRAYER

Get alone with God. Make a list of the top five things you are thankful for and spend some time thanking Him for these good things in your life.

_____

_____

_____

_____

_____

Use this Scripture below to worship God and declare how great He is:

In this the love of God was manifested toward us, that God has sent His only begotten Son into the world, that we might live through Him (1 John 4:9).

Jesus, You are love and You have manifested Your love toward me! Spend some time praying these Scriptures over your life:

Most assuredly, I say to you, he who believes in Me, the works that I do he will do also; and greater works than these he will do, because I go to My Father (John 14:12).

Jesus, You have equipped me for greater works.

…you will say to this mountain, "Move from here to there," and it will move…nothing will be impossible for you (Matthew 17:20).

Jesus, You have made me with a new mindset that nothing is impossible.

ACTIVATION

Begin to write down and talk about the testimonies of what God is doing. For example: people being healed, prayers answered, the good-ness of God revealed. Make declarations about what you desire to see

God do in your city. Ask Him to give you more healings, signs, wonders and miracles.

_____

_____

_____

_____

REMIND YOURSELF TODAY TO VIEW EVERY SITUATION THROUGH YOUR NEW MINDSET THAT "NOTHING IS IMPOSSIBLE."

FURTHER REFLECTION

Read Acts 10:38. Meditate and pray about what the Lord shows you.

DAY 6
MAKING THE PLAY

YOU HAVE THE BALL—AND YOU ARE ON OFFENSE!

People are fully engaging in the pursuit of seeing God's glory cover the earth from a place of authority and assurance. They are no longer satisfied to simply exist in the kingdom of the world; they want to see it transfigure into the Kingdom of our God. (Liebscher, 54-55)

💬 TESTIMONY OF A WORLD CHANGER

Three others and I met up one day after school to discuss how we could ignite change. We wanted to do the unimaginable, not just another after-school program promoting peace and quiet. We were ready to go to war on behalf of our campus and decided to be loud about the way God saved us. We were going to do something different. Something crazy. We prayed and fasted and believed God would have favor on the event.

March 2009 when that bell rang after third period, we played music in the foyer of our high school theater and opened the door with free snacks spread all over the table. My heart dropped to my stomach. Immediately I had my doubts, "I'm just a kid…How can I do this? I'm too fearful. I don't know what to say. They're going to hate it!"

That's when it hit me. This is not about me. I am here to share what God did, and because of what He did, I can do anything.

On Monday, people responded. Tuesday more came. And it grew and grew till Friday when I was the closing speaker. The best message I could think of was one which couldn't be contradicted, and that was my own life story.

Seventy-five people gave their hearts to the Lord that year and we knew my senior year we had to do it again. We prayed and fasted again, believing God would do what only He could. We had a booth set up giving away free "Jesus is Lord" shirts, hats, and Bibles. The people came, and best of all, they stayed. The most important thing we learned that year was the people of this world need love and want it more than anything. So why was I so afraid of sharing about the One who is true love? It was as if they had been waiting their entire life for someone to just tell them the truth.

February 2010, over 2,000 people came to our event in a school about 2,900 students strong, and 467 students gave their hearts to God during school hours! It was one week of obedience to the will of God. And we got every one of their cell phone numbers by telling them to text the word "saved" to a number we set up through Google Voice. As I watched every other student proudly wearing a "Jesus is Lord" shirt at my school, the one thing God did most is help me to realize the change I begged to see had to start in me.

SANDRA RUIZ

DISCIPLESHIP

You have the ball. Jesus has now passed the authority and power of Heaven and earth into your hands. As a world changer, you need to understand Jesus has called you to "disciple nations" (see Matt. 28:19). He has also resourced you for the task ahead:

...All authority has been given to Me in heaven and on earth. Go therefore... (Matthew 28:18-19).

It is time for Christians to stop feeling, thinking, and behaving as though they are insignificant and inferior, and start adopting this new mindset—that we live and breathe to transform our world. The reshaping of your world has been commissioned and backed by God Himself. It is now up to you to move.

Just as the cartoon characters "Pinky and the Brain" would spend their whole lives trying to "take over the world," *you* are called to use your time, energy, and gifts in overcoming the kingdom of darkness with the Kingdom of light. As a world changer, your job description is to discover and develop your God-given dreams, gifts, and talents and use these as channels of His presence. You are called to disciple nations.

Incidentally, discipling nations is not supposed to be a hard task but a joy-filled and thrilling adventure between you and the Lord. Remember Jesus' promise: "…and lo, I am with you always, even to the end of the age" (Matt. 28:20).

As world changers, we have Heaven's commission, supply, and presence by our side *every* step of the way. There is no greater time to live offensively in the Kingdom because we cannot lose in our mission to transform this world.

What do you feel is your unique calling? What do you think God could do with your gifts, dreams, and desires to fulfill your calling and disciple a nation?

What would bring you overwhelming joy and motivation if you surrendered your life to it?

World changers understand their dream of the Kingdom of God invading earth doesn't come by simply sitting around inactive. They know

WHAT IF...*you lived in an offensive mode for God and His Kingdom, with the attitude that you had the ball? Might you make some different choices?*

the ball is in their hands and take steps to co-labor with the Lord and see His desire fulfilled.

What are two things you could do today to shift your life out from a passive mode and into an offensive posture?

_____

_____

CONSIDER THE POSSIBILITIES...if you only lived life fully encouraged

A world changer's number one battle is against discouragement and the sense of isolation. Just as Jonathan and his armor bearer worked together in looking for what God was doing, we, too, are called to be looking for where God is at work—and celebrate, moving toward that.

What are some ways you could ensure that you feed yourself on what God is doing and "fast" from what doesn't seem to be working out?

_____

_____

WHAT IF...You had a joy-filled vision of what God could do through your life?

How might that feel? And how could it translate (or witness) to those around you?

_____

_____

Make a list of three people you can contact who will encourage you as you pursue changing your world. Contact them and ask if you could regularly meet for encouragement and prayer.

_____

_____

Pray and ask the Holy Spirit for more courage and boldness to extend the Kingdom of God in your world.

((•)) PRAYER

Get alone with God. Welcome the Holy Spirit to come and speak to you as you read. Spend some time thanking Him for all the good things in your life.

Use this Scripture below to worship God and declare how great He is:

> *And Jesus came and spoke to them, saying, "All authority has been given to Me in heaven and on earth. Go therefore and make disciples of all the nations…"* (Matthew 28:18-19).

Jesus, You have all authority in Heaven and on earth.
Spend some time praying these Scriptures over your life:

> *And Jesus came and spoke to them, saying, "All authority has been given to Me in heaven and on earth. Go therefore and make disciples of all the nations…"* (Matthew 28:18-19)

Jesus, You have given me all authority to disciple nations.

> *"…and lo, I am with you always, even to the end of the age"* (Matthew 28:20).

Jesus, because You are with me, I can change the world!

ACTIVATION

Imagine a person or situation in your life under the influence of darkness. Ask Holy Spirit what He wants to do in that situation. Make declarations of joy for what He is about to do in that person's life. How does He plan for you to bring Heaven to that person or situation? Do it!

_____

_____

_____

_____

IT'S TIME TO LIVE LIKE YOU HAVE TAKEN POSSESSION OF THE BALL AND ARE ON OFFENSE!

FURTHER REFLECTION

Read First Samuel 14:1-14. What stands out to you? Did you see anything you could glean from Jonathan and his armor bearer's attitude?

Recommended Reading: http://www.revivalorriots.org/archives/1250

IDENTITY SEALED

YOU ARE CALLED TO LIVE WITH A SECURE IDENTITY AS A CHILD OF GOD.

Joshua…refused to be intimidated by the circumstances or culture or voices around him. He rejected the lie that the world around him was greater than the God who was with him. (Liebscher, 57)

💬 TESTIMONY OF A WORLD CHANGER

When I was 12, the separation of my parents was initiated, and by the time I was 17 their divorce had been filed. Those five years were a tangle of drama and heartache, consisting of my father losing his job and returning to alcoholism and my mother crumbling in front of me. Experiencing my loving and safe family fall apart over lost dreams and empty words created deep-seated pain within me. My heart toward my dad became like stone, and all I knew was to be numb.

…Until one day, when I heard God's voice. The simple truths of the Father melted away the years of bitterness, hate, and unforgiveness I had clung to. God swept me up in a vision, and I saw my life play out in front of me. I watched a re-take of different childhood experiences I had gone through from a young age to 19. I saw where my pain was a result of lies I believed. And in these situations I now saw God the Father sitting there beside me, holding and speaking gently to me. He was present every time I felt abandoned and afraid, the times I cried until I

had nothing left, even the times I acted as though nothing mattered, yet I knew I was without a father. Every time, He was there. And then He spoke these simple words, "You were never fatherless." Suddenly this truth illuminated my heart and instantaneous freedom swept through me. I realized at that moment, the world labels us as fatherless but it's the King who calls us His own!

SHANNA

DISCIPLESHIP

In order to secure your identity, you will need to reject the clamor of cultural voices and believe in Heaven's approval. Just as Jesus had to face and overcome the voices of His day, *you*, as a revivalist, are called to live free from the influences of the world.

Satan tried his best to make Jesus believe He wasn't the Son of God. He attempted to trick Jesus into thinking He was insignificant: "…*If* you are the Son of God…" (Matt. 4:3).

The enemy is called, "the accuser of the brethren" (see Rev. 12:10). God tells us to, "Be sober, be vigilant" because the devil roams about like a roaring lion, trying to devour people's identities and restrain them from influencing the planet (see 1 Pet. 5:8). He is simply afraid of our realizing and walking in the truth that we have a mandate and reinforcement from Heaven.

Like Jesus, we can maintain our heavenly position as sons and daughters by rejecting the devil's lies and believing our Father's words: "This is My beloved Son, in whom I am well pleased" (Matt. 3:17).

For what percentage of your day do you think encouraging and empowering thoughts of yourself? How can you increase this?

_____

_____

_____

_____

Do you believe you are God's beloved child, and He is well pleased with you? Why?

_____

_____

Jesus calls you, "the light of the world. A city that…cannot be hidden" (Matt. 5:14). He is proud of you and wants the world to see you! He says, "Nations will come to your light, and kings to the brightness of your dawn" (Isa. 60:3 NIV).

So then, the question is: How do you live a life securely grounded in who God says you are? The answer is simple. You *feast* on His words about you and reject all suggestions of the enemy. Where you have accepted lies, you need to *repent* and think *higher thoughts* of yourself. Ask the Lord to reveal His true definition and design of you, and then step out and walk with the confidence of its reality in your life.

Take a mental stroll through what you mull over in your mind each day. What percentage of your time would be devoted to believing that you are who God says you are? How can you increase this time?

_____

_____

Joshua and Caleb were confident in their identities. They looked at their people and declared of the imposing giants, "for they are our bread…the Lord is with us. Do not fear them" (Num. 14:9). How do you think Joshua and Caleb became so audacious (or composed) in who they were?

_____

_____

Have you ever felt as miniscule as a grasshopper? Ask Holy Spirit to show you a fresh impression or picture of who you really are. Draw or write it down. Then declare this revelation over your life.

_____

_____

Ask Holy Spirit to show you a lie you have believed (or are believing) about your future. Ask Him for the truth. Draw or write it down. Begin to declare the Lord's favor and assurance over your life.

_____

_____

_____

_____

PRAYER

Get alone with God. Welcome the Holy Spirit to come and speak to you as you read. Spend some time thanking Him for all the good things in your life!

Use this Scripture below to worship God and declare how great He is:

Then the seventh angel sounded: And there were loud voices in heaven, saying, "The kingdoms of this world have become the kingdoms of our Lord and of His Christ, and He shall reign forever and ever!" (Revelation 11:15)

Jesus, You reign forever and will take over the world!

Spend some time praying these Scriptures over your life:

Nations shall come to your light, and kings to the brightness of your rising (Isaiah 60:3 ESV).

Jesus, You have called me to shine before nations and kings.

And suddenly a voice came from heaven, saying, "This is My beloved Son, in whom I am well pleased" (Matthew 3:17).

Father, You call me Your beloved son, in whom You are well pleased.

ACTIVATION

Think of some Christians who have greatly affected the world and discipled nations. What was it that caused them to make such a difference?

Begin to pray and ask God to increase your vision for changing a nation. Write down what He discloses to you.

_____

_____

TODAY YOU ARE CALLED TO LIVE WITH A SECURE IDENTITY AS A CHILD OF GOD—AND FROM THIS PLACE YOU ARE FULLY ABLE TO CHANGE YOUR WORLD.

FURTHER REFLECTION

Read Numbers 13:25 to 14:1-10. Think about and pray over the secrets the Lord unlocks to you.

DAY 8
MOUNTAIN HEALERS

YOU ARE CALLED TO TRANSFORM AND HEAL SPHERES OF SOCIETY.

The new breed of revivalist emerging in the earth today will not only stand behind pulpits but will also step into every realm of society…so the land may be fruitful and blessed. (Liebscher, 61)

💬 TESTIMONY OF A WORLD CHANGER

I grew up with a real passion for the outdoors and adventure, and completed my degree in outdoor education. After I wasted most of my teenage years on wild parties and binge drinking, I became a Christian and my world was turned upside down. A desire began to grow inside of me to influence the roughest young teenagers in secular colleges with my passion for the outdoors. So I began to dream and came up with an idea to work with the ten worst boys in each secular high school using my passion for God and camping to turn them around. After planning and preparing with friends, I launched my dream with four schools and 40 of the worst boys. Then I watched the Lord supernaturally bring business people, four-wheel drive vehicles, and volunteers offering their time, resources, and money for the ministry. After only a few weeks, young people began having encounters with Jesus, as did their parents, and their whole lives began to turn around. The program was so successful in its first year that other schools across my state began calling out for us to start it for them. The state government heard about it and decided to finance the rolling out of the program across some of its worst schools in the state. My team is not only changing lives and giving families and teachers hope, but it is also reshaping how the education system handles its most troubled teenagers in Australia.

BROCK, director, SOAR Adventures, age 28

 **DISCIPLESHIP**

The disciples had barely even contributed to the ministry meetings when Jesus was already talking about them "lighting" the world! It began to make sense as, one by one, these ordinary men saw it wasn't just about their little gathering or ministry anymore. They finally awakened to the fact that Jesus had grand plans—larger than they ever imagined! He wanted to change the whole world, and His plan was through using each of them.

Visualize Jesus turning to you and saying, "You are the light of the world, a city that cannot be hidden!" What implication does this have for your life?

_____

_____

_____

Bill Bright and Loren Cunningham's vision of the seven strategic "mountains" or "mind molders" of influence has given Christians a prolific blueprint to impact society with Kingdom wisdom, love, joy, and power (Liebscher, 58-60). God is calling many people out from ministries focused only on the "church," to reaching other particular spheres in the world (e.g., family, religion, economy, education, government, arts and media, science and technology).

> *Our goal is not simply just to get people healed, delivered and saved; it is to bring reformation and restoration to the "ruined cities" (Isa. 61:4). (Liebscher, 60)*

Many Christians have never been told that it is permissible to dream and follow the desires and giftings in their hearts. Often religion can make us all look the same, when in fact God has created you and me wonderfully unique and given us special graces to carry out certain things well. The dreams ingrained upon your heart reside there because God desires to use you to bring revival in the particular realm of society you are zealous about.

> **WHAT IF...***you rejected the cultural voices pervading your life and lived freely as His child and ambassador upon this earth?*

If you could do anything, what would it be?

_____

_____

_____

How does it make you feel to know God is right behind you, not only giving you permission, but also cheering you on?

_____

_____

_____

Patterned after your heart, how would you like to rebuild the ruins of the city (sphere) God is calling you to?

_____

_____

_____

Lance Wallnau says that Jesus told every Christian to "Occupy until He comes. To occupy means to take leadership."[1]

What do you think godly leadership would look like in the area that interests you?

_____

_____

God is extending you an invitation through your dreams and desires. It's
to partner with Heaven and bring healing to that mountain of land...
(Liebscher, 63).

WHAT IF...you believed in your heart of hearts you are a revolutionary? And what if...you lived within that understanding?

Read Second Kings 2:19-22. Imagine what it would have looked like in the city and surrounding villages. How was the enemy stealing from people through this bad water?

_____

_____

_____

Imagine the difference in the entire region because Elisha healed the water. What impact would this miracle have had on people?

_____

_____

_____

WHAT IF...God used you to bring supernatural healing to a body of water in your world today?

Figuratively speaking, what is the body of "stale water" in front of you at this time? What can you pour your "salt" and your "light" into to bring healing and restoration? Ask the Holy Spirit to unpack your next assignment.

_____

_____

_____

Finish your time with the Holy Spirit receiving words of affirmation. Ask who He calls you today.

 PRAYER

Get alone with God. Welcome the Holy Spirit and ask Him to give you spiritual wisdom and revelation.

Use this Scripture below to worship God and declare how great He is:

> ...I will hear from heaven, and will forgive their sin and heal their land (2 Chronicles 7:14).

Jesus, You are the healer of every part of our land.

Spend some time praying these Scriptures over your life:

> The Spirit of the Lord God is upon Me, because the Lord has anointed Me to preach good tidings to the poor; He has sent Me to heal the brokenhearted, to proclaim liberty to the captives, and the opening of the prison to those who are bound (Isaiah 61:1).

Jesus, Your Spirit is on me to bring good news to the poor.

> You are the light of the world. A city that is set on a hill cannot be hidden.... Let your light so shine before men, that they may see your good works and glorify your Father in heaven (Matthew 5:14,16).

Jesus, You believe I can influence the world.

ACTIVATION

What is an activity you currently love doing with others and have favor, grace, and skill in? It could be a sport, art or musical group, social cause, etc. Ask the Holy Spirit to show you what the biggest issue (bad water) is in that pursuit. Now ask Him for something you could do this week to begin to breathe life and change that area.

_____

_____

_____

_____

FREELY DREAM AND STRATEGIZE HOW YOU CAN TRANSFORM THE SPHERES OF SOCIETY GOD HAS CALLED YOU TO.

FURTHER REFLECTION

Read Second Kings 2:19-23. Focus on and pray into what God shows you.

NOTE

1. This information is from a handout from Lance Wallnau, distributed during a Marketplace Transformation Conference at Bethel Church.

DAY 9
REFLECTION SECTION 1

Get alone with God and spend some time receiving His love and affection for you. Ask Him to speak as you reflect over the previous nine days.

As you look over the time, how has your identity grown? Describe how your view of yourself has developed and what this means for your future.

_____

_____

_____

How has your perspective of the Lord matured? Describe some of the changes in how you now see God and what this means in how you relate to Him.

_____

_____

_____

_____

How has your sense of purpose and vision grown? Describe how your purpose and vision have advanced and how this is practically influencing your daily routine.

_____

_____

_____

It is always very important to focus on what God is doing, instead of what He is *not* doing. As we fixate on and give thanks for what He IS doing (every good thing) these testimonies will only increase.

Record some of the miracles and testimonies of what He has been doing in your life over the previous section:

_____

_____

_____

_____

_____

_____

RISKOMETER

How are you doing with stepping out and taking risks for God in releasing the Kingdom? Give yourself a mark on the "Riskometer" scale. (10 = radical risk taker, 1 = not taking any risks.)

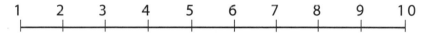

List two areas where you will commit to increasing your level of risk taking for God.

_____

_____

Thank the Lord for all He has done in your life as you worked through the last section.

SECTION 2

UNDER COVERING

DAY 10
UNDER COVER JESUS

YOUR LIFE WILL THRIVE WHEN, LIKE JESUS, YOU SUBMIT TO AND HONOR YOUR COVERING.

I've seen firsthand that when someone harnesses the revelation of covering and submits to spiritual authority, the wind shifts in that person's life. Instead of resistance, he feels the wind accelerating him toward his destiny. (Liebscher, 95)

💬 TESTIMONY OF A WORLD CHANGER

I grew up in Manchester, England in the church my parents planted in 1989. Twenty years on, it's the church they entrusted and empowered me to lead on into its future. As a son I am acutely aware of the privilege of leading something that my parents worked so hard for, invested in, and laid down their lives to do. Everything that I grew up watching them do I have the incredible opportunity to build upon. They modeled to me how to steward the presence of God, to pray for the sick, to hear God's voice, to value and love the poor, to lead with humility, and so much more. My parents believed in me, released me, and allowed me to fail; I was set up to succeed! They influenced and empowered me to lead a church that is moving forward to shape and transform Manchester for the Kingdom of God.

PHIL SMITH, United Kingdom

69

 **DISCIPLESHIP**

Jesus demonstrated the power of honoring and submitting to authority. Even when He was only 12 years old, He modeled how to live under covering. When His parents came frantically searching for Him (after they had left Him at the Temple) the Bible says, "Then He went down with them and came to Nazareth, and was subject to them..." (Luke 2:51). Jesus didn't say, "Hey! I'm the Creator of the world! Give me a break!" Rather, He willingly submitted to their leadership as parents. Because of this, look what resulted from His choice: "And Jesus increased in wisdom and stature, and in favor with God and men" (Luke 2:52). Because Jesus submitted to His parents, God honored and blessed Him with favor in Heaven and on earth!

Imagine being God and submitting yourself to parents, government leaders, soldiers, etc. Why do you think Jesus modeled this for us? What did Jesus want us to have in our lives?

_____

_____

The Father and Jesus also perfectly modeled how a life of covering was to work and what resulted from it. As a son, Jesus demonstrated a heart completely in submission to the authority and covering of His Father in Heaven.

> **WHAT IF...**_your_ _honor of your parents resulted in your life being filled with unparalleled favor and blessing with God and man!_

> *I tell you the truth, the Son can do nothing by himself. He does only what he sees the Father doing. Whatever the Father does, the Son also does* (John 5:19 NLT).

Time after time, Jesus would follow the leading of His Father—moving, ministering, and drawing aside as He was directed. Even when it meant dying an excruciating death on a cross, He said, "...yet not my will, but yours be done" (Luke 22:42 NIV).

Because of this obedience and perfect alignment with His Heavenly Father, Paul tells us the Father rewarded Jesus by raising Him into the highest position of all authority and power that will ever exist. (See Ephesians 1:20-23.) Father God modeled for us the heart of true spiritual covering—not to use and abuse people, but to release and empower them into their unique callings.

The power of what Jesus and Father God did—with Jesus choosing to completely honor His Father's leadership and the Father choosing to radically honor and promote Jesus—ended with not only each of them being blessed, but billions of people on the planet being blessed, too!

WHAT IF...as you honor God, He extravagantly honors you? Have you considered what would happen if we adopted the love modeled in Scripture between fathers and sons? It could change the world!

Jesus is now in Heaven seated in a place of unprecedented authority and power. If God blessed and exalted Jesus, what do you think He will do for us as we lay down our agendas and lives for Him?

_____

_____

_____

((·)) PRAYER

Get alone with God. Welcome the Holy Spirit to come and speak to you as you read. Spend some time worshiping Him for who He is.

Use this Scripture below to worship God and declare how great He is:

Now to Him who is able to do exceedingly abundantly above all that we ask or think, according to the power that works in us (Ephesians 3:20).

God, You are able to do abundantly beyond all that I can imagine! Spend some time praying these Scriptures over your life:

> *But God, who is rich in mercy, because of His great love with which He loved us…and raised us up together, and made us sit together in the heavenly places in Christ Jesus (Ephesians 2:4,6).*

God, You are the one who has extravagantly honored me!

> *So Jesus explained, "I tell you the truth, the Son can do nothing by himself. He does only what he sees the Father doing. Whatever the Father does, the Son also does" (John 5:19 NIV).*

Jesus, You are a perfect Son who is full of honor for Your Father.

ACTIVATION

God's plan for revival is that the increase of His government on earth will never end! God purposes to increase you and your world! Ask Holy Spirit what He is planning to do in your lifetime as you honor your Father in Heaven and your earthly fathers and mothers. Write down what He reveals.

_____

_____

_____

YOUR LIFE WILL THRIVE WHEN, LIKE JESUS, YOU SUBMIT TO AND HONOR YOUR COVERING.

FURTHER REFLECTION

Read the Scriptures and write what the Holy Spirit highlights to you about practical things each of these leaders did to live under covering and blessing.

MOSES AND JOSHUA

- Moses honored Joshua by allowing him draw close to himself and God's presence (see Exod. 33:11). He also taught and instilled wisdom to him (see Num. 27:18; Deut. 31:7; 34:9).

- Joshua honored Moses by fighting, serving, and leading the Israelites into the Promised Land (see Exod. 17:10; 24:13; Josh.11:15).

- God honored this unity between father and son by exalting Joshua as leader, then giving Israel the Promised Land and rest from war (see Josh. 3:7; 11:23).

DAVID AND SOLOMON

- David honored Solomon by training him and leaving him the kingdom of Israel (see 1 Kings 2:1-4,12).

- Solomon honored his father by living for God (see 1 Kings 3:3).

- God honored this unity between father and son with wisdom, wealth, and the Temple. He made Israel the most successful kingdom (see 1 Kings 3:11-14; 10:4,10).

- Even when Solomon sinned, God honored both David and him (see 1 KIngs 11:9-13).

MORDECAI AND ESTHER

- Mordecai honored Esther by adopting her, giving her wisdom, caring for her, and imparting courage in a dire moment (see Esther 2:7,10,11,20; 4:14).

- Esther honored Mordecai by submitting to him, honoring Mordecai to the king, and putting her life on the line for her people (see Esther 2:20,22; 7:3).

- God honored this unity by saving the nation of Israel and exalting Mordecai in the kingdom (see Esther 8:1-2,8,11).

DAY 11
POWER UNITED

YOUR LIFE WILL THRIVE AS YOU HONOR
THE GENERATIONS AROUND YOU.

I am thoroughly convinced that the younger generation needs to understand covering and spiritual authority and that it is impera-tive to be connected to spiritual mothers and fathers if we are going to be victorious. (Liebscher, 75)

TESTIMONY OF A WORLD CHANGER

Three years ago, my grade-eight daughter started a prayer group on her junior high campus. I met with another mom and prayer-walked the school early in the morning once a week to support them and see God move on the campus. Brenna faithfully continued the weekly prayer group the next year. This year we ordered the "Jesus Culture Campus Awakening Kit," and she started bringing prayer and power to her campus. Her group grew from 4 to 16 kids, who are beginning to see themselves as world-changers and history-makers! They are taking prayer out of the room and into the halls and learning to risk and believe God for more! In the last few weeks, they have seen knee pain healed and a girl who was injured in PE class comforted as they stepped out in prayer! They have even been approached by a teacher for prayer.

SUZIE

 **DISCIPLESHIP**

It is true there is a supernatural victory released on the earth when fathers and mothers unite with sons and daughters. Moses and Joshua illustrated the power of this unity between the generations. An impressive picture of Moses and Joshua's accord was their battle and victory over the Amalekites (see Exod. 17:8-16). The Israelites only won when Moses held his rod into the air while Joshua and the army fought with their swords. The generations required each other to overcome. Moses provided the authority and power, while Joshua contributed the courage and skill to administer the work of the Lord.

> *There was a combined release of authority and blessing in the midst of the battle because of the way Moses and Joshua interacted. The result of their convergence was victory. (Liebscher, 75)*

When generations work together in honor, unity, and humility, God gives favor and establishes the Kingdom on earth. Why do you think He chooses to bless and release favor when the generations work together?

_____

_____

_____

What do you think would have happened to Israel if the Joshua generation chose to fight alone, without the covering of Moses?

_____

_____

_____

What are some current battles your spiritual fathers or mothers are in? How can you support and serve them better at this time?

_____

_____

Moses was an incredible father because he believed in Joshua and loved him. Moses wanted him to succeed. As a father to his mighty warrior, you can imagine Moses being one of Joshua's greatest fans and supporters. I love how the Bible says, "So Joshua defeated Amalek and his people with the edge of the sword" (Exod.17:13). Here we see that even though Moses' involvement

> **WHAT IF...**_you not only live for what God has called you to do, but lay your life down to help your fathers and mothers achieve their dreams?_

was absolutely essential for the Israelites victory, as a great father, he gives the credit and honor to Joshua. It's almost like he builds a platform for Joshua to stand on to launch him into his God-given destiny.

Moses embodied the Kingdom of God by loving and honoring Joshua above himself. As Paul wrote, "Be kindly affectionate to one another with brotherly love, in honor giving preference to one another" (Rom. 12:10).

WHAT WOULD BE POSSIBLE FOR THE FUTURE OF THE WORLD...if we united the generations like Moses and Joshua?

What sort of a father or mother does it take to be able to lift the younger generation up to their ceiling and say, "You go, now! Take it even further"?

_____

_____

_____

_____

PRAYER

Get alone with God. Welcome the Holy Spirit to come and speak to you. Today, thank Him for being a great Father to you. Think of all the good things He has placed into your life and worship Him for who He is.

Use this Scripture below to worship God and declare how great He is:

Jesus Christ, the faithful witness, the firstborn from the dead, and the ruler over the kings of the earth. To Him who loved us and washed us from our sins in His own blood (Revelation 1:5).

Father, You honor Your sons greater than anyone.
Spend some time praying these Scriptures over your life:

And he will turn the hearts of the fathers to the children, and the hearts of the children to their fathers… (Malachi 4:6).

Jesus, You will restore the hearts of the generations so they unite.

And it shall come to pass in the last days, says God, That I will pour out of My Spirit on all flesh; your sons and your daughters shall prophesy, your young men shall see visions, your old men shall dream dreams (Acts 2:17).

Jesus, Your Spirit will unite the generations to change the world.

ACTIVATION

Ask Holy Spirit for an encouraging prophetic word or picture for your spiritual father or mother. Write it down and deliver it today. Spend some time praying and declaring the goodness of God over them.

_____

_____

_____

YOUR LIFE WILL THRIVE WHEN YOU HONOR THE GENERATIONS AROUND YOU.

FURTHER REFLECTION

Read Exodus 17:8-13. Meditate and pray upon the things the Lord illuminates.

LIFE THROUGH HONOR

HONORING YOUR SPIRITUAL COVERING RELEASES LIFE AND PROTECTION FOR YOU.

> *Covering brings benefits! …You don't need to spend your life striving on your own when you can build upon what your fathers and mothers have already established. The choice is yours. (Liebscher, 68)*

💬 TESTIMONY OF A WORLD CHANGER

My wife and I have always lived with a high priority of generosity. The Lord did amazing miracles of provision throughout our whole lives; however, it was constantly hand to mouth. We gave liberally, considering our income, but never got ahead and experienced abundance. We had picked up some debt from mistakes as well as life itself.

I remember thinking of our dear friends in the church who walked in an unusual anointing for more than enough. They had a financial favor—like the "Midas touch"—where everything they touched turned to gold.

Recognizing the God-given anointing on their life, we acknowledged and honored it. My wife and I approached them and asked if they would impart to us the ability to carry it—if they would lay hands on us and pray. They prayed very simply, pointedly, and powerfully. I don't even know how to describe what happened because there was nothing dramatic, yet everything dramatically changed and I can trace it back to that night. Suddenly we were becoming exposed to more than enough. There was now more than we needed for the next decision, the next month, or the next need. And seven or eight years on, it remains this way.

Out of our testimony, we were enabled to pray in faith for others who have been completely released from debt. I believe the Lord is equipping us to recognize favor on another person, honor it, and receive from them. In our particular case it was the laying on of hands that transferred the anointing, but I don't know if it always has to be that way. Regardless, the Lord used it powerfully and I'm glad.

BILL, Senior Pastor

 ## DISCIPLESHIP

The Kingdom of God is the life of God: "…righteousness, peace and joy in the Holy Spirit" (Rom. 14:17). When the life of God enters a city it always flows through people who honor God and each other. First Peter says:

Likewise you younger people, submit yourselves to your elders. Yes, all of you be submissive to one another, and be clothed with humility, for "God resists the proud, but gives grace to the humble" (1 Peter 5:5).

As the fathers and mothers honor the sons and daughters and the sons and daughters honor the fathers and mothers, the life and grace of God begins to surge into their world.

The word *honor* in the Bible is the Hebrew word *kabad*, which means "to be heavy."[1] In other words, to honor someone is to attribute a sense of weightiness, solidness, high respect, or great esteem. It is when we look beyond the grit and focus on what is "golden" and precious. When we excavate the things in one another that are "weighty," we usually find the Kingdom of God. It is as we recognize and call out the gold in our fathers and mothers—and the fathers and mothers recognize and call out the gold in the sons and daughters—that the life of God ensues.

On a scale of one to ten (one being *no* honor, ten being consistent honor), how do you rate how well you honor your parents? How do you feel they honor you?

_____

_____

What happens when you focus on the "gold" in your fathers and mothers instead of the "dirt"? How does it change how you relate to them?

_____

_____

Write a father or mother's name below, and next to their name list five honorable qualities they possess.

_____

_____

It is amazing how many people I meet who are getting thrashed in life because they have no covering. The spirit of independence has separated them from covering and community, and darts are striking and hurting them. It's not really that complicated. If it's raining and you don't wish to get soaked, then jump under an umbrella. Spiritual covering provides protection from the storms of life. (Liebscher, 99-100)

IMAGINE...the security of being surrounded and protected by godly fathers and mothers. How empowered would your life be?

_____

_____

If God prefers that we be supported by others, why would the devil conspire to isolate us?

_____

_____

Some of the biggest mistakes from past world changers were made at the end of their lives, when they thought they knew better and stepped away from spiritual input and covering. What can you do to prevent yourself from making the same mistake?

> **WHAT IF...**
> *encompassing yourself with a spiritual covering was going to accelerate you into your destiny?*

_____

_____

PRAYER

Again, position your heart in the "secret place" with God and begin to worship Him. Do something different. For example, dance, sing, go for a walk in nature, etc. Spend time thanking Him for all the good things in your life.

Use this Scripture below to worship God and declare how great He is:

> *And that He will set you high above all nations which He has made, in praise, in name, and in honor, and that you may be a holy people to the Lord your God, just as He has spoken* (Deuteronomy 26:19).

God, You are the God of honor who establishes honor on the earth. Spend some time praying these Scriptures over your life:

> *Therefore we also, since we are surrounded...let us lay aside every weight, and the sin which so easily ensnares us, and let us run with endurance the race that is set before us* (Hebrews 12:1).

Jesus, You surround me with a family of strength so I can run the race set before me.

Likewise you younger people, submit yourselves to your elders. Yes, all of you be submissive to one another, and be clothed with humility, for "God resists the proud, but gives grace to the humble" (1 Peter 5:5).

Jesus, You pour out grace on me when I am humble.

 **ACTIVATION**

Personal victory also comes through proper partnership with those who hold the rod of God. Who is a spiritual father or mother you could learn and grow from? Make a plan to meet and glean from them.

_____

_____

CHOOSE TO HONOR YOUR SPIRITUAL COVERING AND RELEASE LIFE AND PROTECTION FOR YOURSELF TODAY.

FURTHER REFLECTION

Read Hebrews 12:1-17. Think upon the things God shows you.

NOTE

1.   *"Kabad," Blue Letter Bible Lexicon,* accessed February 28, 2012, http://www. blueletterbible.org/lang/lexicon/lexicon.cfm?Strongs =H3513andt=NASB.

GRACE OVERFLOWS

HONORING YOUR SPIRITUAL COVERING RELEASES COURAGE AND WISDOM FOR YOU.

> *The principle of submission to authority is simply that all people,*
> *in every generation, are called to be under authority. In fact we*
> *cannot walk in authority without being submitted to authority.*
> *(Liebscher, 74)*

💬 TESTIMONY OF A WORLD CHANGER

Recently I was faced with one of the toughest situations I've ever had to walk through. I had to confront a close friend on an issue, bring it into the light, and risk losing that relationship in the process. I knew what was in front me and it was the right thing to do, but I lacked the courage to fully walk it out. However, what I did have was a strong covering in my life who was able to impart wisdom and insight into what I was facing. When I had doubts, they assured me I was doing the right thing. When I felt afraid and overwhelmed, they comforted and reminded me everything would be okay. When I was staring down what I thought to be an impossible situation, the covering in my life gave me perspective and courage to respond correctly. I believe there is a grace that enters your life when you trust those who have gone before you and allow them to speak into your heart. Challenges that feel impossible alone become opportunities to grow closer to the community around you— and you discover strength you didn't realize you had.

DEREK

 **DISCIPLESHIP**

The principle of submission to authority is simply that all people, in every generation, are called to be under authority (Liebscher, 74).

Peter said, if a group of people adopt this kind of humble lifestyle, they will be prime targets for God to pour out the riches of His grace.

Likewise you younger people, submit yourselves to your elders. Yes, all of you be submissive to one another, and be clothed with humility, for "God resists the proud, but gives grace to the humble" (1 Peter 5:5).

The riches of His grace include increase in areas such as courage, wisdom, protection, and identity.

COURAGE

Courage is contagious. When a brave man takes a stand, the spines of others are stiffened. (Billy Graham, quoted in Liebscher, 96)

When sons and daughters submit to their elders or those in authority, they receive courage. Esther was emboldened when she deferred to the insight and wisdom of Mordecai. A divine grace of courage flowed through Mordecai and into her heart. God wants to impart boldness into your life, a supernatural bravado that will cause you to stand up and save nations!

WHAT COULD YOU ACHIEVE...if you lived a life fully encouraged by your spiritual fathers and mothers?

WISDOM

There is experience and wisdom that can only come from years lived. (Liebscher, 74)

One of the most significant attributes we can receive from yielding to our elders is wisdom. Elders are people who have usually lived long and effectively, causing them to carry a grace of wisdom. Just as Joshua "was full of the spirit of wisdom, for Moses had laid his hands on him" (Deut.34:9), so, too, can you receive an impartation of the grace of wisdom to lead and change your world through the fathers and mothers God has placed around you.

Reflect on times in your life when you gained courage or wisdom from an elder or person in authority. How did it give you grace to succeed in that area?

_____

_____

_____

_____

_____

IDENTITY

A child doesn't decide his or her name; the parents do. (Liebscher, 101)

Many young world changers lack identity because their spiritual fathers and mothers have never named them. In biblical times, it was the role of the parents to "describe" a child through their choice of a name. There is something powerful when you align yourself under a Moses, Elijah, or Mordecai and they begin to call out the greatness in your life.

> **WHAT IF...***God has special grace reserved for families who live by the principle of honor?*

Who do your spiritual fathers or mothers call you?

_____

_____

_____

_____

How do you think for yourself and hear from God while still submitting to authority and allowing your fathers and mothers to speak into your life?

_____

_____

_____

_____

_____

_____

_____

PRAYER

Get alone with God. Welcome the Holy Spirit and thank Him for all the good things in your life.

Spend time reading these Scriptures and declaring them over your life. Highlight any words that stand out to you and talk to God about what He is saying.

> God decided in advance to adopt us into his own family by bringing us to himself through Jesus Christ. This is what he wanted to do, and it gave him great pleasure (Ephesians 1:5 NLT).

Jesus, You are the builder of the best family!

> Those who have been born into God's family do not make a practice of sinning, because God's life is in them. So they can't keep on sinning, because they are children of God (1 John 3:9 NLT).

Jesus, Your life is flowing through my family!

> Joshua…was full of the spirit of wisdom, for Moses had laid his hands on him… (Deuteronomy 34:9).

Jesus, You impart wisdom into my life through my covering.

THE RELATIONSHIP CIRCLE: WHO IS ON THE INSIDE?

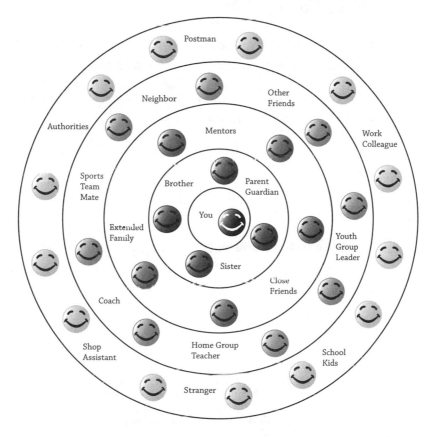

Every person is under the influence of someone; we just need to make sure we are being led by the God-appointed people. A world changer understands it is very significant who we have closest to us in our inner circle. Therefore, it's fundamental to invite and network people strategically into our lives who we can learn from and submit our lives to.

1. Fill in each of the circles, placing those who are closer and more influential to you in the inner circles (For example, best friend, parents, spouse, etc.) and those who have less personal input in the outer circles.

2. Highlight those who have the *most* access, impact, and guidance for you.

3. Is there anyone in your inner circles you feel is a negative influence?

4. Who are two or three people who could be spiritual fathers or mothers in your inner circles? Include their names also.

5. Put down two to three people you are going to offer spiritual mentoring and support to this year.

6. Spend time praying for those in your inner circles as well as for the ones you are going to lead.

 ## ACTIVATION

Ask the Holy Spirit to show you an area of your life you need to submit to a leader's wisdom and authority so you can receive the grace that comes from Heaven.

_____

_____

HONORING YOUR SPIRITUAL COVERING RELEASES COURAGE AND WISDOM FOR YOU.

FURTHER REFLECTION

Read Genesis 1:28. Consider what God blessed the first family with the ability to do. Spend a few minutes thanking Him for your family, friends, and faith community.

DAY 14
ALIGNMENT

GOD HAS SPIRITUAL FATHERS AND MOTHERS FOR YOU TO COME UNDER THE COVERING OF.

If young people and young leaders can put fathers and mothers in a place of honor in their hearts, the rest will work out. (Liebscher, 83)

TESTIMONY OF A WORLD CHANGER

I grew up in a family that discouraged needing each other. We were all very independent. It was important you could do things on your own without relying on others. When I married and moved away, I discovered that being able to do things "on your own" didn't mean you were strong; it meant you were isolated, and being disconnected wasn't fun! I quickly realized I needed and desired to be a part of a community. My husband and I prayed God would bring people in our lives to be a covering for and a community around us. He answered our prayer. Once we got connected to a community, our life drastically changed. It was almost like I didn't have to fight so hard for breakthrough. I didn't need to strive anymore. There was an extra grace in our lives because we were able to draw from the strength of those around us. Now, it's so clear to me why God created us to live in community. He wants to surround us with grace and strength.

BECKY JOHNSON

 **DISCIPLESHIP**

Sometimes we are looking for the perfect fathers or mothers to serve, and fail to see God has already placed men and women around us who we can learn and grow from. He has hand chosen spiritual fathers and mothers for us to submit to, honor, and serve.

World changers know that in these last days God is turning the hearts of the fathers to the children and the children to the fathers (see Mal. 4:6). They also know they can grow and learn from any person or situation God places them in. As a world changer, you need to believe God has ordained men and women to release the benefits of covering in your life, but not all the people He has assigned you will be famous (Liebscher, 86).

Do you think it is possible for God to use people in your community to spiritually lead and guide you despite their imperfections? Why?

_____

_____

_____

_____

Do you see evidence of Malachi 4:6 in your life? For example, do you sense the fathers and mothers around you turning toward you and your heart shifting toward them? Describe what is happening.

_____

_____

World changers know they can receive covering and benefit from more than one father or mother. With today's technological advantages, we can follow and extract from people all around the world. The Internet and print and social media are all powerful platforms for us to receive from these amazing men and women.

However, there is another level of covering that only comes from having personal, consistent contact with someone. "We need more in our lives than a national leader with whom we have no chance of fostering a relationship" (Liebscher, 87).

Fathers and mothers were meant to guide, but in order for them to invest in and counsel us, we need to be able to know each other intimately. True fathering is up-close and personal—where there is communication, feedback, questions and answers, serving and being empowered, as well as opportunities for being released.

Make a list of five things your "up-close and personal" spiritual fathers and mothers can bring into your life?

_____

_____

_____

_____

_____

What activities could you do with your spiritual fathers and mothers to deepen your relationship and maturity?

_____

_____

What areas of your life could you be more open and honest about with your spiritual fathers and mothers?

_____

_____

_____

_____

DAVID AND MEPHIBOSHETH: FROM ORPHANS TO SONS

Often, people walk around with a defeated *orphan spirit* which tells them, "Nobody loves me; everybody hates me!" The orphan spirit prefers us isolated and desperate when we were actually called to live and feast at the King's table. God is raising up fathers and mothers to bring sons and daughters into the royalty they were created for.

Read Second Samuel 9:1-13. What stood out to you?

_____

_____

How did Mephibosheth think of himself? (See verse 8.) How do you view yourself? Are there any negative thoughts you should repent of?

_____

_____

How do you think David saw Mephibosheth? How do you think King Jesus sees you? Ask Jesus for three words or pictures that describe how He sees you.

_____   **WHAT IF...**_a spiritual_

_____   _father such as David_

_____   _came into an area of_

_____   _your life today that was_

_____   _dry, like a desert? What_

could God do through

a father like him?

How does it make you feel that Jesus, the King of all kings, has come into your wasteland and sent for you to dwell in His royal palace? Begin to worship and thank Jesus for rescuing you and redeeming your authentic identity as a royal heir in the Kingdom.

_____

_____

Begin to pray for your spiritual fathers and mothers to be blessed with wisdom and favor like King David. Make declarations of blessing over them and their lives, families, and calling.

_____

_____

((·)) PRAYER

Get alone with God. Welcome the Holy Spirit to come and speak to you as you read.

Spend some time thanking the Lord for all the good things in your life. Read the Scriptures below and ask Holy Spirit for pictures of who He wants to be to you today.

> *You are the helper of the fatherless* (Psalms 10:14).

> *...But to put their hope in God, who richly provides us with every-thing for our enjoyment* (1 Timothy 6:17 NIV).

Jesus, You are my helper and richly provide everything for my enjoyment!

> *How precious also are Your thoughts to me, O God! How great is the sum of them!* (Psalms 139:17)

Jesus, You think I am amazing and You never stop thinking that!

ACTIVATION

If you don't have a spiritual father or mother, pray and ask God to raise up mothers and fathers in your life, and position your heart to esteem those He has already brought to you.

WHY NOT BEGIN TO PRAY, LOOK FOR, AND COME UNDER A FATHER OR MOTHER'S COVERING TODAY?

FURTHER READING

Read Second Samuel 9:1-13 and meditate and pray about the things that God shows you.

DAY 15
REFLECTION SECTION 2

Get alone with God and spend some time receiving His love and affection. Ask Him to speak to you as you reflect over the previous five days.

How has your understanding grown in regards to the importance of spiritual covering?

_____

_____

_____

_____

_____

_____

_____

What are the main keys you will take from this section and put into practice in your life?

_____

_____

_____

_____

_____

_____

_____

What are some things you are excited about the Lord doing in and through you in the near future?

_____

_____

_____

_____

_____

How has your view of God and His Kingdom grown? Describe some of the changes in how you now see God's vision for the generations working together.

_____

_____

_____

_____

_____

How could you work better with the generations in establishing a long-lasting influence of His Kingdom in your world? Dream about the next hundred years!

_____

_____

_____

_____

_____

_____

Remember it is always very important that we focus on what God is doing, not on what He is not doing. As we concentrate on and give thanks for every good thing He is doing, these testimonies will only increase.

Record some more miracles and testimonies of what the Lord has been doing in your life over the previous section:

_____

_____

_____

_____

_____

RISKOMETER

Give yourself a mark on the "Riskometer" scale regarding how you are doing with stepping out and taking risks for God in releasing the Kingdom. (10 = radical risk taker, 1 = not taking any risks.)

```
 1     2     3     4     5     6     7     8     9    10
 |--+--|--+--|--+--|--+--|--+--|--+--|--+--|--+--|--+--|
```

List two areas where you will commit to increasing your level of risk taking for God.

_____

_____

Spend a few minutes thanking God for all He has done in your life over the last section.

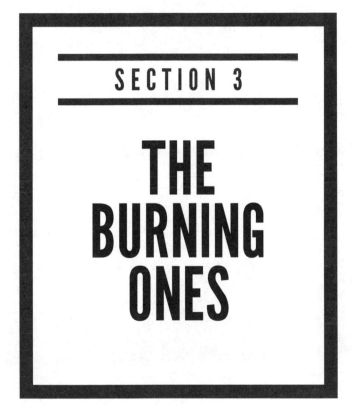

SECTION 3

THE BURNING ONES

DAY 16
EXPERIENCING LOVE

GOD IS NOT ANGRY WITH YOU BUT WANTS
YOU TO ENCOUNTER HIS LOVE DAILY!

Too many people are content to live a life of information rather than revelation. But knowledge alone will never inflame a sustained blaze in you to love Jesus passionately. Only revelation will do that. (Liebscher, 120)

TESTIMONY OF A WORLD CHANGER

As a young world changer, I boldly evangelized and prayed for people, but was guarded in my personal relationships. I had memorized many verses about the love of God, but found I could only trust God to a certain point. I believed in His identity as Healer, Savior, and Deliverer, but had not experienced the love of the Father in a way that made me feel my heart was a treasure to Him. One day, while I was playing music with some friends, emotions of being cherished and loved overwhelmed me so much I began to weep. It felt as though my heart was being tenderized. I sensed how much the Lord cared about my heart, my thoughts, and my desires. From that moment forward, I was only seconds from tears any time I thought about the love of God for me. After that day, I found myself being vulnerable with people and connecting to them more intimately. I discovered myself loving people without concern of rejection

99

and serving others' needs. Sitting and listening to people became like intimate worship with the Lord.

JOHN, businessman, age 23

 DISCIPLESHIP

There is a major difference between knowing something as information in your head and *experiencing* it. Many Christians today are content to live their lives stopping at the information that God loves them rather than encountering His love. God is real and desires intimacy and relationship with every son and daughter in His Kingdom. His plan is to compel us all into a lifestyle where we continuously live in His love.

WHAT COULD HAPPEN...if you continuously had encounters with God's immeasurable love for you?

Paul prayed that every believer would be given, "...power...to grasp... and to know this love that surpasses knowledge" (Eph. 3:18-19 NIV). He prayed God would supernaturally dispense the "grace" and ability to encounter the limitless love of God. Paul knew if everyone could partake of God's love, they would be, "...filled to the measure of all the fullness of God" (Eph. 3:19 NIV). He recognized a direct connection to God's children having a personal revelation of His love for them and living in His fullness of life on earth.

Today there is a new breed of world changers who are taking time aside to receive God's love for them so they can live in and release His abundance.

Think back to a time when you felt the love of God. Write how it happened and how it impacted your life. In what way did it change and empower you?

_____

_____

_____

WHAT DO YOU THINK...the fullness of God would look like in a human being? How much of God could one person handle?

Think of stories of people who have walked closely with God and seen His fullness manifest in their lives.

_____

_____

_____

The enemy has tried to convince God's children to believe He is continuously angry with them. A view of God that says, "He is angry and out to punish you," has sadly held believers captive by fear and insecurity, causing many to be powerless in changing their world. However, the enabling truth about God Is He has never stopped loving you. It was *He* who stepped out first, sending His only Son to die for you, and if, "He who did not spare His own Son, but delivered Him up for us all, how shall He not with Him also freely give us all things?" (Rom. 8:32). God *longs* to give you His fullness and all things in the Kingdom so you can change your world.

HOW EMPOWERED WOULD YOU BE...if you walked in the complete assurance that God was never angry or disappointed with you?

Where do you think the image of an angry God has come from? What do you think the fruit of this image of God is in a believer's life?

_____

_____

What will separate or stop God's love for your life?

_____

_____

_____

Because of this fact, how can you now begin to dream and live?

_____

_____

_____

_____   **WHAT IF**...*God was*
                                         intensely passionate
_____   *for you to achieve your*
                                         dreams and desires?
_____

_____

_____

((•)) PRAYER

Get alone with God. Welcome the Holy Spirit to come and speak to you as you read.

Use this Scripture below to worship God and declare how great He is:

> *For the Lord God is a sun and shield; the Lord bestows favor and honor; no good thing does he withhold from those whose walk is blameless. O Lord Almighty, blessed is the man who trusts in you* (Psalms 84:11-12 NIV).

Jesus, You are a good God who bestows good things on me! Spend some time praying these Scriptures over your life:

> *There is therefore now no condemnation to those who are in Christ Jesus, who do not walk according to the flesh, but according to the Spirit* (Romans 8:1).

Jesus, You don't condemn me today, but You are for me.

> *I am convinced that nothing can ever separate us from God's love...nothing in all creation will ever be able to separate us from the love of God that is revealed in Christ Jesus our Lord* (Romans 8:38-39 NLT).

Jesus, You and I are inseparable because You love me.

 **ACTIVATION**

Spend a few minutes talking with Father God about all your dreams and desires. Tell Him the things you love doing and some of the questions you have about life and the world. Ask Him to continue to reveal His love in your life.

_____

_____

_____

_____

REMEMBER, GOD IS NOT ANGRY WITH YOU. HE REALLY WANTS YOU TO ENCOUNTER HIS LOVE.

FURTHER REFLECTION

Read Romans 8:31-39 with eyes looking for God's goodness and love. Write down what the Holy Spirit highlights.

SUSTAINED PASSION

TO SUSTAIN PASSION FOR GOD YOU HAVE TO ENCOUNTER HIS LOVE EVERY DAY.

It is achievable to live a life that escalates in passion year after year. The new breed of revivalists emerging in the earth is experiencing the long burn of love, not just the short burst of an experience that quickly fades away. (Liebscher, 115)

💬 TESTIMONY OF A WORLD CHANGER

While in college, I was working at the university library. I had recently encountered God's love and begun to see Him manifest His power through my life in supernatural ways. While I worked, I would play worship music in my headphones and constantly be worshiping God in my heart. Others around me would play games or browse the Internet, keeping up with social networking posts, but I was overwhelmed with the ever-present God who was my closest friend. Even on my breaks, I would go downstairs into the library stacks where I could be alone in the dark to worship the Lord in song and dance and receive of His presence. I dreamt of the great things God wanted to do in and through my life—visualizing things like traveling the world seeing people healed. Today, my heart is still burning for Jesus and to see the world encounter His love.

KRIS, itinerant minister, age 26

 **DISCIPLESHIP**

Sustained passion flows from His love for us.

> *Deep inside every Christian is a desire to live thoroughly in love with Jesus. Bill Johnson says this is why Jesus is called the "Desire of the Nations" (Haggai 2:7). Every person on the planet desires Jesus; they were created for Him, they just don't know it. Jesus is the perfect fulfillment to the deepest yearnings of the human heart. (Liebscher, 114)*

To live a life escalating in passion for Jesus year after year is achievable. Many times, however, Christians have "left their first love" (see Rev. 2:4). They temporarily reignite it by attending conferences and other inspiring events, but they are usually never given the right keys to maintaining a heart ablaze for Him. Their zeal for the Lord fluctuates because many times they are taught to invest longer hours in prayer, stop sinning, and read their Bible more. However, by themselves these spiritual disciplines don't contain the anointing. And world changers require Heaven's power to transform the world!

Have there been times you have felt more in love with God than other times?

_____

_____

Have you ever tried to stir up your longing for Jesus by doing more good works or spiritual disciplines? What was the result? Why?

> **WHAT IF...***it is* **God's love for us that** *actually sustains our* **passion for Him?**

_____

_____

_____

John says, "We love Him because He first loved us" (1 John 4:19). When John implored us to return to our first love (see Rev. 2:5) he was telling us to revisit the revelation that God first loved us. *It's the knowing of His love for us that awakens our desire for Him.* When you encounter His all-consuming love for you, the natural response is to be completely enamored with Him. His love incites ours, to the point where we don't have to strive or struggle to remain captivated. It just comes naturally (Liebscher, 116).

> *Look at me. I stand at the door. I knock. If you hear me call and open the door, I'll come right in and sit down to supper with you. Conquerors will sit alongside me at the head table, just as I, having conquered, took the place of honor at the side of my Father. That's my gift to the conquerors!* (Revelation 3:20-21 MSG)

What happens to your passion when you realize God is completely in love with you?

_____

_____

DID YOU KNOW...you are intimately entwined within His heart?

How does it make you feel, knowing that even your best attempts to earn God's devotion will never sustain your passion, but simply stopping and receiving His radical love for you will reignite your hunger for Him?

_____

_____

WHAT IF...God has never stopped pursuing you as fervently as He did before you were saved?

World changers are arising all across the earth with a sustained passion for God because they are encountering and receiving His love for them daily. They deliberately devote time to stop, wait, and be filled with God's love for them. As they drink of His love, something activates (or kindles) inside them. They are taken from encounter to encounter, and as they nurture this cycle of love their affection and passion increases.

Jesus often "withdrew into the wilderness and prayed" (Luke 5:16). How difficult do you think it was for Jesus to withdraw from the needs around Him to be with His Father? Why? What motivated Him to do it?

_____

_____

WHAT IF...you actually became more effective and influential, not from working, but from spending time in His presence?

What do you think Jesus' prayer times involved? What do you suppose He received from God?

_____

_____

WHAT IF...instead of structuring your life around the busyness of the world, you lived in harmony with God's desire and calling for you to be with Him?

List two ways you will begin to structure time into your day when you can be with God and receive His love. Make a commitment to take time to abide in His love for you, and tell a friend who can help remind you to be accountable to your promise.

_____

_____

PRAYER

Get alone with God. Welcome the Holy Spirit and thank Him for all the good things in your life.

Use this Scripture below to worship God and declare how great He is:

Behold, I stand at the door and knock. If anyone hears My voice and opens the door, I will come in to him and dine with him, and he with Me (Revelation 3:20).

Jesus, You are the God who wants to come in and dine with me. Spend some time praying these Scriptures over your life:

To him who overcomes I will grant to sit with Me on My throne, as I also overcame and sat down with My Father on His throne (Revelation 3:21).

Jesus, You have made me to overcome and sit in a place of rest.

My flesh and my heart fail; but God is the strength of my heart and my portion forever (Psalms 73:26).

Jesus, You are the strength of my heart forever!

 ## ACTIVATION

Plan an outing with God. Set aside some time and plan to get alone by yourself with Him. Take some things you love to do such as music, art, drawing, or journaling. Then worship, pray, and receive His love. Ask the Father to tell you how He feels about you. Ask Him what He likes about you, and ask Him to tell you some of the names He calls you. Receive His love, kindness, and praise.

TO SUSTAIN YOUR PASSION FOR GOD YOU HAVE TO CHOOSE TO RECEIVE HIS LOVE EVERY DAY.

FURTHER REFLECTION

Read Luke 5:16, Matthew 14:23, Mark 1:35 and 6:46. What was Jesus' strategy to be able to stop and pray?

DAY 18
ONLY YES

EVEN IN THE MIDST OF DISTRACTIONS, YOU ARE CALLED TO SAY YES TO JESUS.

There is something powerful that happens when people say yes to Jesus in the midst of distractions. (Liebscher, 121)

💬 TESTIMONY OF A WORLD CHANGER

I was raised in a Christian home and gave my life to Jesus at the age of four. I went to church every week with my family, attended a Christian school, believed in Jesus, but never really knew what it meant to surrender my life completely to Him. Even though I was a Christian, my high school years were spent playing sports and hanging out with my friends, but not really surrendered for God. At the age of 17, I responded to an altar call for a message preached one Sunday night. Kneeling at the altar, I told God, "If I'm going to do this Christianity thing, I'm going to give 100 percent." Everything changed for me in that moment. My life became consumed for Jesus. My passion…my focus…my decisions. I knew He had called me to great things and my life was to be spent completely on Him.

BANNING

 **DISCIPLESHIP**

The Christian life is easy when we abide from a continuous revelation of His love. However, we live in an imperfect world constantly "warring" against us being in the secret place with God. Our society offers the average person an unparalleled amount of distractions like television, mobile technology, the Internet, movies, travel, sports, and stuff...oh so much stuff! While these distractions are not evil in themselves, if we do not learn to master them, they will steal our ability to dwell in His love (Liebscher, 120-121).

How do you think Jesus would respond to the world we live in? How would He interact with the many options and distractions we face?

_____

_____

_____

How do you feel you should respond to the clamor of life?

_____

_____

_____

Christianity wasn't meant to be a guarded life constantly saying *no*, but a life of freedom overflowing with *yes*. We have an incredible opportunity, in this world of clutter and chaos, to say yes to Jesus. Submerged within an exhausting number of options, one of the most indicative and loving things we can do in our lives is to choose to surface and be with Jesus.

> *When we say yes to Jesus in the midst of distractions and options, it establishes a deep conviction inside of us which cannot be easily shaken.*
> *(Liebscher, 121)*

It is this simple but significant daily choice that ignites God's power in our lives and multiplies the Kingdom within and through us.

While we do not look at the things which are seen, but at the things which are not seen. For the things which are seen are temporary, but the things which are not seen are eternal (2 Corinthians 4:18).

Saying yes to Jesus is a positive goal. Jesus is calling us to draw close so He can ignite us with His fiery love (Liebscher, 117).

Have you ever made the choice to say yes to Jesus in the middle of incredible options? What did it do inside you?

_____

_____

_____

How do you handle times when you make the wrong choice and opt for the interruption and seduction of the world? What do you do with condemnation?

_____

_____

_____

TURNING YOUR AFFECTIONS TOWARD HIM

Whether it is your daily devotional time or throughout your busy day, the issue is this: Will you turn your attention and affection to Him? As important as it is to have a dedicated daily time with the Lord, it is not the ultimate goal. The objective is to have the affections of your heart pointed in His direction no matter what is going on (Liebscher, 123). Today's world changers understand the power of slowing down and positioning themselves in God's love, asking Him questions, and waiting for understanding.

What does it mean to you to "turn your affections toward Him?"

_____

_____

Marriage is a powerful union because it happens in the midst of options. (Liebscher, 121)

What are some of the options you have in your life that can divert you from intimacy with Him?

> **WHAT IF...***you began to say yes to Jesus over these distractions? What could God do in your life?*

_____

_____

_____

_____

Write down three ways you could slow down, even during your work or study, and focus on the Lord.

_____

_____

PRAYER

Get alone with God. Welcome the Holy Spirit and thank Him for all the good things in your life.

Use this Scripture below to worship God and declare how great He is:

For love is as strong as death, jealousy as cruel as the grave; its flames are flames of fire, a most vehement flame. Many waters cannot quench love, nor can the floods drown it... (Song of Solomon 8:6-7).

God, You are the One whose love for me is stronger than death. Spend some time praying these Scriptures over your life:

But you, when you pray, go into your room, and when you have shut your door, pray to your Father who is in the secret place; and your Father who sees in secret will reward you openly (Matthew 6:6).

Jesus, You are the One who wants me to be alone with You.

While we do not look at the things which are seen, but at the things which are not seen. For the things which are seen are temporary, but the things which are not seen are eternal (2 Corinthians 4:18).

Jesus, You have called me to live focused on Your heavenly Kingdom.

MARRIAGE COVENANT: SAYING YES

Get alone with God. Spend some time unraveling any complications and congestion in your heart and wait on God's presence. Center your devotion toward Him and allow Him to reveal His love to you. Thank Him for His faithfulness and kindness in your life.

Welcome the Holy Spirit to come and speak to you as you read.

_____

_____

 ## ACTIVATION

Write God a letter describing how much you love Him. Thank Him for the amazing things He is doing in your life.

Dear Jesus:

_____

_____

_____

_____

_____

Love from _____

The moment you look up and are in a place of affection with Jesus the Heavens are opened. (Smith Wigglesworth, quoted in Liebscher, 123)

TODAY, EVEN IN THE MIDST OF YOUR DISTRACTIONS, TAKE TIME TO SAY YES TO JESUS.

FURTHER READING

Read First Corinthians 13:4-8. Then replace the word "love" with "Jesus" and read it out aloud to yourself. What did the Holy Spirit highlight to you about God?

DAY 19
IDENTIFIED!

YOU ARE CREATED TO LIVE FROM THE PLACE WHERE FATHER GOD DEFINES AND VALIDATES YOU.

As this new breed of revivalist begins to encounter the passionate love of Jesus and entwine their hearts intimately with Him—as He becomes the most important Person in their lives—their view of themselves begins to change dynamically. (Liebscher, 127-128)

💬 TESTIMONY OF A WORLD CHANGER

One night while in worship at a youth camp, God came to me and took me away in a vision. He explained why He had created me the way He had, from my hair color all the way to my feet. Each physical characteristic was designed by purpose—with love.

He said my eyes were blue because of how I saw others…He had gifted me to be discerning and see through people. He said I was muscular with strong legs because He formed me to be able to withstand hard things. He even explained all the way to my feet.

This affected the way I lived because it helped me understand I could never be down on myself when God had fashioned me a certain way— on purpose. It made me view who I was differently, and I could see myself from His perspective.

SEAJAY

👥 DISCIPLESHIP

God passionately wants to reinforce your true identity. He is determined about this because He knows if you believe you are a child of God, you will shape nations. Your identity in Him is the most important thing He wants you to know—that you are His beloved, His chosen one, and the love of His life.

> Our perceptions of ourselves manifest in the way we live life. If you believe there is greatness in you, your life will demonstrate that reality. (Liebscher, 128)

If we look at the life of Jesus, we can conclude that even from a young age, and then throughout His life, He received affirming words about His identity because God was constantly speaking to Him.

- When He was only 12, He believed He was God's Son: "Did you not know that I had to be in My Father's house?" (Luke 2:49 NASB). It seems that from a young age, Jesus was receiving messages from God that secured His identity as God's Son.

- Then as Jesus began His ministry, the Father continued to reinforce His true identity. When He was baptized, a loud voice from Heaven was heard, "You are My beloved Son; in You I am well pleased" (Luke 3:22).

- Then, later on the Mountain of Transfiguration, God spoke again, "This is My beloved Son, in whom I am well pleased" (Matt. 17:5).

Because Jesus heard and believed He was God's Son, He was empowered to live as a Son of Heaven and release Heaven into the earth.

WHAT IF...*God thought you were better than you ever imagined?*

What are some of your earliest memories of God's voice? How did it shape your identity and purpose in life?

_____

_____

WHAT COULD YOU ACTUALLY BE CAPABLE OF...if you truly began to believe who God says you are?

Just as the Father spoke identity to Jesus throughout His life, so does He desire to speak into your life, "You are my royal son, and I am pleased with you."

As a world changer, you need to make time to listen for and accept God's affirmation of who you are. This is very important because when the One who first conceptualized you and spoke you into being is given room to express His opinion about who you are, then His voice will displace the judgments and persuasions of other people and the enemy. You will gaze into the looking glass of His heart and truly see yourself as He sees you (Liebscher,127-128). And when you recognize who you really are, you will be empowered to change the world.

How often do you invite the Father to express His love messages over you? How do you think this is affecting your life and purpose?

_____

_____

WHAT COULD HAPPEN...if you lived like God's words over your life were truer than your circumstances and what other people say about you?

PRAYER

Get alone with God. Welcome the Holy Spirit to come and speak as you read. Spend some time thanking Him for all the good things in your life. Use this Scripture below to worship God and declare how great He is:

In the beginning was the Word, and the Word was with God, and the Word was God. All things were made through Him, and without Him nothing was made that was made (John 1:1,3).

God, You create everything through Your Word.
Spend some time praying these Scriptures over your life:

Your words were found, and I ate them, and Your word was to me the joy and rejoicing of my heart; for I am called by Your name, O Lord God of hosts (Jeremiah 15:16).

Jesus, Your words give me joy, and I am called by Your name!

…This is My beloved Son, in whom I am well pleased (Matthew 17:5).

Jesus, You call me Your beloved son today.

 ## ACTIVATION

Think about your life. What kinds of "junk food" are you feeding your soul and identity with? Ask Holy Spirit to show you what television shows, movies, Internet sites, negative people, etc. are unhealthy for you. Plan a spiritual junk food fast to remove negativity and untruth from your spiritual diet. In the same way, focus on indulging in a buffet of sweet, spiritually wholesome food!

YOU ARE CREATED TO LIVE FROM THE PLACE
WHERE FATHER GOD IDENTIFIES YOU.

FURTHER REFLECTION

Before Adam and Eve fell into sin, whose voice and words did they listen to? What did God say over them in Genesis 1:28 and 31?

GOD'S SONS AND DAUGHTERS

YOU ARE A CHILD OF GOD.

Banning, you have a choice. You can either choose to be a preacher or a son. If you choose to be a preacher, you will be good sometimes, and other times you won't be that good. But if you choose to be a son, you will always be good, because you are a fantastic son. (Liebscher, 133)

🗨 TESTIMONY OF A WORLD CHANGER

With tears streaming down my face, I told my mentor why my father was sent to jail when I was a child, how this caused me to grow up bitter, angry, and enslaved to shame. I had never known an earthly father, so I couldn't even begin to comprehend I had a heavenly Father, whose love was extravagant for me. I harbored overwhelming doubts and fears in trusting Daddy God. I had believed the lie I wasn't "good enough." I thought He could love everybody else but me and assumed He was angry with me. In that moment of transparency, the Lord quietly drew me in close, whispering softly to my broken heart, saying, "I am the Father to the fatherless. I am the Father you can trust. I am that Father who never left you. I am the Father who loves you unconditionally, no matter what." A beautiful invitation was extended to me that day, into a walk with my Daddy God, and He has proven Himself to be One who is faithful to His promise. I can trust Him with everything I have and know His extravagant love is for me.

COURTNEY, 19

DISCIPLESHIP

When we pause to really think about what Jesus has done for us and rest in the power of all He achieved for us, there is nothing that should shake or hold us back. Jesus has made you God's son or daughter, and because He has accomplished this work, there is very little you can do to mess it up. It's time to believe you are an amazing child of God...and to rise and walk as one.

Yet to all who received him, to those who believed in his name, he gave the right to become children of God (John 1:12 NIV).

Why is it important to look to Jesus' performance for our identity and not our own? What happens when we look at *our* accomplishments as a barometer for our identity?

_____

_____

_____

You are a magnificent child of God. Let those words soak deep into your spirit. If you can really believe you are a fantastic son or daughter of God, something unwavering and victorious will take place in your life.

You are not wonderful because of anything you alone have done or will do. Not one tiny part of your exploits has made (or ever could make) you a son or daughter of God. You are an

> **WHAT IF...***Jesus has completed your righteousness and made you like Himself? What if...you are better than you ever imagined?*

extraordinary child because *the* extraordinary Son of God stepped into your shoes, destroyed your old sinful life, and raised you up to be with Him in the royal palace. Jesus did it all, from start to finish. It was *His* performance that has sealed the deal forever. Jesus is "…the author and finisher of our faith" (Heb. 12:2).

How much do you think your performance could add to what Jesus has done on the cross?

_____

_____

What confidence does it give you knowing Jesus is the "author and perfecter of your faith"? How do you access Jesus' grace?

_____

_____

YOU HAVE THE KING'S BLOOD

Royalty is who you are! Now because of Jesus, you have royal blood and the King's DNA. You are now "reborn—not with a physical birth…but a birth that comes from God" (John 1:13 NLT). You sit on a heavenly throne and have heavenly desires, heavenly motivations, and heavenly authority, all because of Jesus. Just because you may have a bad day and do something wrong, it doesn't change what Jesus has accomplished in you. You are still "seated…with Him in the heavenly places in Christ Jesus" (Eph. 2:6 NASB).

When you truly repent and believe "it is all Jesus," an internal security and strength settles into your heart, and you are established to impact nations!

It is done—the work has been completed—you just have to believe it!

> *You are of God, little children, and have overcome them, because He who is in you is greater than he who is in the world* (1 John 4:4).

Many Christians become anxious they have lost their salvation or are "lesser sons" when they make mistakes. Have you ever felt like that? What is the truth regarding your identity, even when you mess up?

_____

_____

WHAT IF...when we failed or sinned, instead of beating ourselves up, we cleaned off our debris, asked God to forgive us, and moved on—living as sons and daughters should?

When you believe you are a son, you believe you have access to Heaven's abundance and can release it on earth. You are aware there is more than enough. You know in every situation God has an answer and He yearns to extend the life, joy, and peace of Heaven.

How much resource do you believe Heaven has? Is there a situation that Heaven cannot respond to or resource?

_____

_____

How much resource do you believe you have access to? Ask Holy Spirit to show you how much of Heaven you have at your disposal.

_____

_____

Read Galatians 4:6. What is the difference between how a son operates compared with a slave? What benefits does a son have that a slave does not?

_____

_____

Spend some time thanking God as a child would thank his or her father. Ask Him to help you pray and live like His very own—and not as a slave or orphan.

PRAYER

Get alone with God. Welcome the Holy Spirit to come and speak to you as you read. Worship God by declaring who He is. Underline parts in these Scriptures that stand out to you and begin to pray them over your life.

Use this Scripture below to worship God and declare how great He is:

"And I will be a Father to you, and you shall be sons and daughters to Me," says the Lord Almighty (2 Corinthians 6:18 NASB).

God, thank You for looking after me as a Father.
Spend some time praying these Scriptures over your life:

But to all who believed him and accepted him, he gave the right to become children of God. They are reborn—not with a physical birth resulting from human passion or plan, but a birth that comes from God (John 1:12-13 NLT).

God, You have made me your son or daughter!

Because you are sons, God has sent forth the Spirit of His Son into your hearts, crying out, "Abba, Father!" Therefore you are no longer a slave but a son, and if a son, then an heir of God through Christ (Galatians 4:6-7).

Jesus, thank You that your Spirit is in my heart and I am a son and heir of Heaven.

ACTIVATION

John G. Lake had a remarkable appreciation of the sonship of the believer. He would train his "healing students" to visit the home of a terminally ill person. So confident in their identity, he told them not to come back until the person was healed. They all went out believing who they now were and saw the terminally ill healed! Heaven breathed life through their revelation, trust, and obedience. Ask the Holy Spirit to identify the sickness of a person He wants you to release healing over today. Be on the lookout and available to step out as a child of God. Be expectant to witness the authority you have in Jesus.

_____
_____
_____
_____

TODAY, LIVE LIKE YOU ARE YOUR FATHER'S SON OR DAUGHTER... AND RELEASE HIS GOODNESS IN YOUR WORLD!

FURTHER REFLECTION

Read Matthew 14:19-21, John 2:7-10, and Luke 4:40. What stood out to you about these miracles?

DAY 21
LOVING FATHER, NOT EMPLOYER

GOD VIEWS YOU AS A BELOVED CHILD—NOT AN EMPLOYEE.

> God is not our boss in Heaven just barking out orders for us to
> follow. He is a loving Father who longs to partner with His children.
> He sent His only Son to die on the cross—not to gather employees,
> but to establish a love relationship with people. *(Liebscher, 132)*

TESTIMONY OF A WORLD CHANGER

As the recipient of three graduate degrees and the owner of a 150-employee company, most of my life has revolved around performance. I found my worth and sense of significance through what I could accomplish. Even my spirituality was tied to disciplining myself to obey biblical principles, perceiving Jesus as a taskmaster whom I had to please. From the ages of 19 to 31, I drifted away from any dedication to Jesus, but He never gave up on me. Slowly drawing me back, He showed me His love and care in powerful ways. After a divorce 37 years ago, He supernaturally brought me my wonderful, godly wife, Kaylinn, which started me down the path of fully understanding His love. As Christ's ambassador, she loved me when I was not very lovable. Though at times I still struggle with unhealthy performance, my heart's desire is to live moment by moment, resting in Christ's incredible love for me, with my accomplishments flowing from a response to His love and my position as His son.

DOUG, businessman

DISCIPLESHIP

Many Christians view God as "a boss" who is yelling orders and over-looking their performance with a big stick. Unfortunately, this concept of God reduces their connection with Him to that of an employee. However, it could not be farther from the truth. God is not like a cold and disinterested taskmaster, scrutinizing your every move. He is not abusive, forceful, or constraining. Nor is He emotionless and relationally disconnected from us. He actually sent His Son so we could become a part of the communion and intimacy of the Trinity. God desires us to be as up-close and personal with Him as He is with Himself—Father, Son, and Holy Spirit. He will not be satisfied with anything less than a relationship with you in which you do not work *for* Him but *with* Him. You are not "hired"—you are in love with an impassioned, devoted, and sentimental God.

> **WHAT IF...***the Lord was more interested in partnering with you as His child instead of you working for Him?*

What do you think causes a person to see himself as an employee of God instead of a beloved son or daughter? What is the root issue?

_____

_____

Try to imagine the intimacy God calls you into. Is it possible to keep relating to Him as an employee? Why not?

_____

_____

In a world where most people have not had a father, let alone another person who fully knew how to express their love for them, it can often be hard for us to connect with the Lord's invitation of intimacy. Many would prefer to work for God rather than seemingly "waste" time receiving His affection and love. But God is not like our earthly fathers, bosses, teachers, or anyone else who may have demanded performance over relationship. He is the God who yearns to *know* us before we *do* anything for Him.

WHAT IF...God passionately desires relationship over performance?

In First John 3:1, we see God's original intention for us as His children— not workers:

> *Behold what manner of love the Father has bestowed on us, that we should be called children of God!*

He is the resolute Father who fixes His gentle gaze on you and awaits your attention and affection. He is eager to lavish you with gifts of royalty. He desires to open doors of opportunity for you and hear you sing! God is your closest confidant and will settle for nothing less than your transparency! Today's world changers know their effectiveness and power to impact the world can only be generated through continuous dependency on and pursuit of their Father. It is from this foundation they can truly transform their worlds.

Have you ever felt like God was only interested in your performance? What was the fruit of this? Have you ever felt the passionate pursuit and love of God? What fruit resulted?

_____

_____

WHAT IF...the Kingdom of God is filled and extended with "...righteousness and peace and joy" (Rom. 14:17) because He is your loving Father, not your employer? (See Matthew 18:1-4.)

Why does God fervently approach you, tenderly lead you, and generously shower you with gifts? What does He want to take place in your life?

_____

_____

How does this make you feel toward Him?

_____

_____

Write a love letter from God…to yourself.

Welcome the Holy Spirit and ask Him to speak through you as you write a letter. Using a clean sheet of paper, begin to write a devoted Father's letter from His heart to yours. Start the page as you think He would. For example, "My dearest one…." Allow His warm and embracive thoughts to inspire your words.

When you have finished, read aloud what He says. And thank Him for His lavish love for you.

_____

_____

_____

_____

_____

_____

_____

_____

_____

From _____

(•)) PRAYER

Get alone with Your Heavenly Father. Welcome the Holy Spirit to speak as you read. Make a list of the top five things you are grateful for and spend some time thanking Him for these good things in your life!

Use this Scripture below to worship God and declare how great He is.

Now may our Lord Jesus Christ himself and God our Father, who loved us and by his grace gave us eternal comfort and a wonderful hope, comfort you and strengthen you in every good thing you do and say (2 Thessalonians 2:16-17 NLT).

Father, You are my greatest advocate and champion.

Spend some time praying these Scriptures over your life and your world:

For I am convinced that neither death nor life, neither angels nor demons, neither the present nor the future, nor any powers, neither height nor depth, nor anything in all creation, will be able to separate us from the love of God that is in Christ Jesus our Lord (Romans 8:38-39 NIV).

Father, You yearn for closeness and sweetness in our relationship!

How precious also are Your thoughts to me, O God! How vast is the sum of them! If I should count them, they would outnumber the sand. When I awake, I am still with You (Psalms 139:17-18 NASB).

Father, You can't stop thinking about me and never leave me alone!

ACTIVATION

Ask the Holy Spirit, "Who is on Your heart right now that You want me to pray for?" Allow Him to lead you in your prayer. Ask Him for specific people groups in your school or workplace, your community (or even globally) that He wants you to intercede for and follow His lead in these prayer times. Release a revelation of the love of God into the lives of people you know.

_____

_____

_____

_____

ALLOW FATHER GOD TO RELATE TO YOU AS YOUR MOST TRUSTED CONFIDANT, RELIABLE PROVIDER, CARING GUARDIAN, AND STRONGEST PROTECTOR.

FURTHER REFLECTION

Read Luke 15:11-24. And contemplate the steadfast encircling of the Father's love.

DAY 22
THE ANSWER

GOD DESIRES TO RELEASE HIS ANSWER THROUGH YOU INTO YOUR WORLD AND MAKE A DIFFERENCE.

Every day, all around us, people are experiencing a famine of love and power…. They are searching for an answer and that answer resides in you. (Liebscher, 137)

💬 TESTIMONY OF A WORLD CHANGER

I was on a trip with some friends in a foreign country. We were aiming to release healing and signs and wonders. I unfolded out of the car and told an interpreter, "Follow me." Walking boldly up to a food stand where four young men were having a drink, I asked, "Ummm, this might sound a bit strange, but is anyone here sick? Jesus is healing lots of people at the moment." The four men replied, "No, but that guy over the road is sick and needs prayer." I looked up to see a man on crutches with a knee brace. I said, "Come with me. You are about to witness Jesus heal this man." So the young men followed me and moved toward the man on crutches. I asked the man what was wrong with his leg, and he began to tell me about numerous knee and hip operations. So I asked one of the young men to put his hand on the man's knee and say, "Jesus heals you." As soon as one of the young men did this, the man on crutches opened his eyes wide and said, "More, more. Up here, up here!" pointing to his hip. I got another of the young men to release healing in Jesus' name.

The man's knees and hip were instantly healed and all five people gave their lives to Jesus on the street. Then the one who had been on crutches walked across the street, leaned his crutches up against his food stand, and went back to work completely healed!

DAVE, writer, age 37

DISCIPLESHIP

Everywhere we turn, people are wounded and hurting. They desperately need healing and hope. And marvelously, the solution resides in you!

Just like the story of the four lepers in Second Kings 7:3-11, there is a famine in the earth today because the enemy has besieged and pillaged people's lives. Sickness, poverty, depression, and hopelessness are rampant as dear souls are held captive and unable to break free.

The good news is, Jesus defeated the enemy and now has the power to release people from their bondage. Ephesians 4:8 says, "When He ascended on high, He led captivity captive, and gave gifts to men." In other words, Jesus has overthrown the powers that keep people captive, and He wants to give out gifts to all men. Where there is sickness, Jesus has gifts of healing available. Where there is poverty, He holds prosperity. And where there is depression and hopelessness, He comes to restore dreams and delight!

Today's new breed of world changers understands that people are enslaved by a "dead and defeated enemy" and Jesus can revolutionize any circumstance because He is Lord!

If the enemy is invalidated and Jesus wants to give "gifts" to all men, what is stopping you from bringing salvation and restoration into your world?

_____

_____

_____

_____

_____

What are some stories of miracles, healings, and signs and wonders which inspire faith and hope that Jesus has won the victory?

_____

_____

_____

Those in famine, will always listen to those with food. (Liebscher, 138)

Today's world changers understand it is not a day to hoard the bounty of Heaven's resources and keep silent, but "now is the day of salvation" (2 Cor. 6:2). It is your day to announce that victory and provision is available to all in need. Freely you and I have received, so freely we are required to give (see Matt. 10:8). Just as the four lepers realized, "we are not doing right. This day is a day of good news, and we remain silent" (2 Kings 7:9), it is your time to fully comprehend the benefits Jesus has given you, and liberally pour out on those in need. It is your privilege to heal the sick, cleanse the lepers, raise the dead, and cast out demons.

The world is incarcerated in spiritual drought. How deeply ravenous and despairing do you think they are?

_____

_____

What do you have that the people in your world are desperate for?

_____

_____

Take some time to visualize yourself walking in your true identity—healing the sick, cleansing lepers, raising the dead, and casting out demons.

How vast and boundless is the love of God for you today? What are the implications for your life, having a Father who loves you so much?

_____

_____

_____

Who is inside you? How does this understanding affect every issue you see in your world?

> **WHAT IF...***Jesus Himself is living and breathing inside you today? What could He accomplish through your life?*

_____

_____

_____

_____

From what position do you normally live:

1. The outside in—focused on issues and circumstances and how they affect you?

2. The inside out—focused on the risen Christ and His love, Heaven's endless resources, and how He hopes to affect your world?

How can you live more from the inside out?

_____

_____

_____

Because Jesus walked fully confident in His Father's love, He moved in power without doubt that His Father would answer His prayers. Ask the Holy Spirit if there are any lies you believe about how Father God feels regarding you today. Repent of these misconceptions and ask Him how He truly feels about you and sees you. Write down the truth and pray this over your life.

_____

_____

_____

IMAGINE WHAT IS POSSIBLE...if God is for you, and His answer resides in you. Who or what can be against you?

PRAYER

Get alone with God. Do something different with the Lord this morning—sing, dance, shout praises, lie quietly and soak. Just enjoy Him before you start your day's routine.

ACTIVATION

Spend some quality time soaking in the presence of God, receiving His joy, peace, and righteousness. Ask Him what "gifts" He desires to release today in your world—through you—and whom He wants you to bring those gifts to.

_____

_____

POUR OUT FROM ALL YOU HAVE INSIDE OF YOU...AND CHANGE YOUR WORLD!

FURTHER REFLECTION

Read Ephesians 3:14-21. Meditate and pray about the things that God shows you.

Recommended reading: *From Comfort Zone to Performance Management* by Alasdair White

DAY 23
REFLECTION SECTION 3

Get alone with the Lord and spend some time receiving His love and affection for you. Ask Him to speak as you reflect over the previous eight days.

As you look over this last section, what was a common theme the Holy Spirit highlighted for you to learn and mature from?

_____

_____

_____

_____

In what ways have you grown in your understanding of God's love for you? How has this affected your heart and life?

_____

_____

_____

_____

How has this time changed your view of who you are and what you are capable of?

_____

_____

_____

_____

What are the top three things you are going to do to stop and take time to receive God's love?

_____

_____

_____

_____

Record some more miracles and testimonies of what the Lord has been doing in your life over the last eight days.

_____

_____

_____

_____

_____

_____

RISKOMETER

Give yourself a mark on the "Riskometer" scale regarding how you are doing with stepping out and taking risks for God in releasing the Kingdom. (10 = radical risk taker, 1 = not taking any risks.)

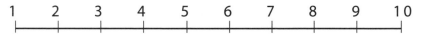

List an area where you will commit to increasing your level of risk taking for God.

_____

_____

Thank Him for all He has done in your life over the last section.

SECTION 4

THOSE WHO PRAY

IMPACTING PRAYER

SPENDING TIME WITH GOD IN FELLOWSHIP GREATLY IMPACTS SOCIETY!

All the resources and dominion of Heaven are available to us as we pray…. And all over the world, in every part of society, He is raising up prayer in the midst of darkness. (Liebscher, 143)

💬 TESTIMONY OF A WORLD CHANGER

Our city is a college town and Halloween had become more like a festival where literally thousands of people would come into the city to party. The origins of this holiday are based around false worship and celebrating darkness. God put it on my heart to release true worship to the King in our city on this day. So a group of us had an idea to rent a theatre in town and use art and music to worship in spirit and truth. We had a couple of worship bands and various expressions of art throughout the night. Many people came and life was released over our city! There were many stories of what God did that night. One of my favorites was this guy who randomly ended up in the theatre. He didn't know Jesus, but as he encountered the presence of God he was compelled to give his life to the Lord, right there by himself without anyone even sharing with him.

ZACK

 **DISCIPLESHIP**

Every great movement of God can be traced to a kneeling figure.
—D.L. Moody[1]

This is not another section in a book to give you the latest formula on prayer. My goal isn't to put any more pressure on you, but what I hope to accomplish is to help you recapture a vision that your Father in Heaven desires to meet with you. It is as simple as that. I feel a burden that, like no other time in history, God is calling His children to Himself because He hopes to meet with and love on them. Prayer is not primarily motivated by the incredible purposes it can achieve, but it is first and foremost God wanting to be with you.

Jesus lived upon this cornerstone of prayer. He constantly withdrew just to be with His Father to receive His love, to talk with Him, and to feel His presence. Today, I hope you begin to capture a conviction that will shape the rest of your life: God waits for you in the secret place, not for ministry but just to spend time with *you!*

When you think about prayer, what does it mean to you?

> **WHAT IF...**_your_ _intimate times of fellowship with the Lord were all that was needed to radically alter the lives of people and situations all around the world?_

Considering that your Father just wants to meet His child in the secret place, how could you return to the simplicity of prayer?

History is filled with stories of people who were consumed by simple fellowship with God and from this had a notably extensive impact on society. Take for example:

- Frank Bartleman—the intercessor for the Azusa Street Revival

- Dr Paul Yonggi Cho—the South Korean pastor who spawned the world's largest church with 1,000,000 members.[2]

- Heidi Baker—a Californian woman who is consumed with the secret place and has seen over 10,000 churches planted in Mozambique and 10,000 people fed daily!

You were created to impact nations through prayer. Jesus said, "You are the light of world" (Matt. 5:14), but your prayers are not only to light up your personal life but also to illuminate the world!

IMAGINE IF...your prayers changed the world's nations, stopped earthquakes, eradicated slavery and disease, and released angels and the resources of Heaven into situations!

Your prayers are precise and effective (see James 5:16) and they hold the potential to profoundly impact society. World changer...it is time to start praying!

What situations or injustices do you hope to see changed in the world today? Knowing your simple fellowship with God can transform circumstances, how does this motivate you to pray to see Heaven released in this situation?

God has placed His people strategically around the world with the intent to transfuse it with His Presence through our lives. Contrary to popular opinion, politicians, Hollywood, or the media do not determine where our world goes. Christians lead it through the influence of prayer, love, and faith-filled actions.

WHAT IF...there are situations and circumstances the Lord is waiting for you to step up and pray into so Heaven's victory is released today?

_____

_____

_____

What would it look like to see "all the families blessed" in your sphere of influence?

_____

_____

_____

What areas of society do you feel passionate about God influencing? For example, sports, arts, government, science and technology, family, business and economics?

_____

_____

_____

PRAYER

Get alone with God. Welcome the Holy Spirit and thank Him for all the good things in your life.

Use this Scripture below to worship God and declare how great He is:

I will wait for You, O You his Strength; for God is my defense (Psalms 59:9).

Jesus, You are powerful and You have given Your power to me. Spend some time praying these Scriptures over your life:

And not only that, but we also rejoice in God through our Lord Jesus Christ, through whom we have now received the reconciliation (Romans 5:11).

Jesus, You desire our prayer time to be filled with joy.

> *Do you not know that you are the temple of God and that the Spirit of God dwells in you?* (1 Corinthians 3:16)

Jesus, You have moved into me and today Your Spirit lives in me.

 ## ACTIVATION

What are two areas where you are naturally in a place of influence? It could be a family, sports team, interest group, art program, or a band. Think about the two main issues in that group. Commit to pray into those situations to release new attitudes, healing, prosperity, unity, etc. How could you steward this opportunity as a leader to make that group the best place to be?

_____

_____

SPENDING TIME IN FELLOWSHIP WITH GOD GREATLY IMPACTS SOCIETY!

FURTHER REFLECTION

Read Acts 3:25-26. What stands out as you read? Who are the sons of the prophets and what are they going to do?

NOTES

1. D.L. Moody, quoted in "Inspirational Prayer Quotes," Hannah's Cupboard, accessed March 03, 2012, http://hannahscupboard.com/prayer-quotes.html.

2. "O Come All Ye Faithful," The Economist, November 01, 2007, accessed March 03, 2012, http://www.economist.com/node/10015239.

THE SECRET PLACE

YOU ARE CALLED TO ESTABLISH A SECRET PLACE WHERE YOU AND GOD CAN MEET.

There are some things you cannot get in public; you must press in for them in private. You can't go to conferences…to get this anointing. It is an anointing that results from encountering God in the secret place, the inner room of prayer. (Liebscher, 148)

💬 TESTIMONY OF A WORLD CHANGER

My first memories of talking to God were as a young child. We lived in the country, so there were plenty of sprawling trees to climb and take in the amazing views around you. I didn't even know what I was doing, but I would talk to Jesus and feel such peace and life while I would just sit there. It is only now I understand what I was experiencing was His presence. Little did I recognize this action would set in motion my passion for the secret place.

As a teenager, I really began to seek God along with my family and friends. During my quiet times, I used my Bible and a devotional book called Streams in the Desert by L.B. Colman. This fueled the desire to be with God more and more, and eventually the voice of God became a very normal part of my life.

One night at a youth service during worship, I encountered the Lord in a vision. Jesus and I were in an expansive green meadow with rolling hills

all around. Jesus was simply holding my hand, leading me through the
meadow. Every few moments He turned to me although never uttering
a word. He simply smiled, and I was filled with overwhelming peace and
love for Him. Many years later, I am still visiting that secret place He gave
me as a source of wisdom and strength.

LESLIE CRANDALL

DISCIPLESHIP

Jesus was a man of prayer and had a secret life with the Father. Luke remembers, "But Jesus Himself would often slip away to the wilderness and pray" (Luke 5:16 NASB).

Mark also comments on the Lord's routine: "Now in the morning, having risen a long while before daylight, He went out and departed to a solitary place; and there He prayed" (Mark 1:35).

I am encouraged when I see thousands of young people seeking God together, but what I want to know is if this is happening in their bedrooms when no one else is looking.

> *But you, when you pray, go into your room, and when you have shut*
> *your door, pray to your Father who is in the secret place; and your*
> *Father who sees in secret will reward you openly* (Matthew 6:6).

Jesus tells us the greatest place of reward is when we go away by ourselves, leave all other influences and distractions behind, and pray to our Father in private. He told us that if we are just after the public "show business" of prayer, then we only receive public reward. However, He says when we get into the secret place with our Father, He rewards us. Jesus had a secret place His Father saw, and His prayer life is still being rewarded by God today!

Why is it important to be "alone" with God, "shut the door," and pray in secret?

_____

_____

_____

What do you think is the difference between a reward from man and a reward from God?

_____

_____

_____

Whenever we find ourselves drifting away from the ultimate reason we are alive—to love God and be loved by God—the secret place realigns our priorities with His heart (Liebscher, 152). Everyone needs to find their own secret place. For some it is a closet, for others a mountain

> **WHAT IF...**_being alone with God was the highlight of your day?_

view, for some it's driving in their car, and for others it is getting up early and walking. Your secret place may not be an exact location, but you enter it when you pull away from the world and find a place you and the Lord can establish a personal history together (Liebscher, 148). As a world changer, if you are to step into your destiny, you need to find a place where your foundation of love can be expanded wider than anything else in your life.

What does your secret place look like? Where do you withdraw from the world and connect with God most easily?

_____

_____

_____

_____

How great is the calling the Lord has placed on your life? In order to sustain His design, how much more should you build a foundation of His love?

_____

_____

_____

FIND A SECRET PLACE OF POWER

There are some things you cannot find in public; you must press in for them in private. One of the most powerful areas we can develop in our lives is intimacy with God. Thanks to Jesus, we have been invited into the most cherished relationship where God now calls us "sons" and "friends" (see John 15:15). Just as spending time alone with someone develops intimacy, God loves it when we separate to Him, unravel our hearts, and communicate with Him.

Before you start your day, remember the primary purpose of prayer is fellowship and intimacy with God. Spend at least a half to two thirds of your time today receiving His love, worshiping, and thanking Him for all He has done.

WHAT IF...a secret place allows you to be real, specific, and honest with God?

Take a few minutes to ask the Holy Spirit, "Am I believing any lies about myself that the world has tried to put on me?" Repent of this and then ask the Holy Spirit, "Who do *You* say I am?" Write the words and pictures He shows you.

WHAT IF...it opens the door for Him to release abundant grace to change vital areas of your world today?

How willing do you think Jesus is to bring Heaven into your world?

_____

_____

_____

_____

WHAT COULD YOUR WORLD LOOK LIKE...if Heaven invaded it?

Ask Jesus more specific questions about issues you and your community are facing. Pray and declare over those areas the detailed pictures and truth He shows you.

_____

_____

_____

((•)) PRAYER

Get alone with the Lord and thank Him for all the good things in your life.

Use this Scripture below to worship and declare how great He is:

> No longer do I call you servants, for a servant does not know what his master is doing; but I have called you friends, for all things that I heard from My Father I have made known to you (John 15:15).

Jesus, You are the God who desires and calls me friend.
Spend some time praying these Scriptures over your life:

> Jesus said to him, "You shall love the Lord your God with all your heart, with all your soul, and with all your mind" (Matthew 22:37).

Jesus, You want us to have a love relationship.

> But you, when you pray, go into your room, and when you have shut your door, pray to your Father who is in the secret place; and your Father who sees in secret will reward you openly (Matthew 6:6).

Father, You have called me to depart to a solitary place with You.

ACTIVATION

Challenge yourself to get up 30 minutes earlier each day to spend time in the secret place and ask God specific and intimate questions about your life and His. Ask the Holy Spirit, "Who is on Your heart?" and "Who should I pray for today?" Allow Him to lead you in your prayer times.

TODAY ESTABLISH A SECRET PLACE WHERE YOU AND GOD CAN MEET.

FURTHER REFLECTION

Read Matthew 6:5-13. What is God's reason for you having a secret place and exclusive time with Him? What does He want to do?

DAY 26
PERSISTENCE PAYS

YOU ARE CALLED TO CONSISTENTLY PRAY FOR YOUR WORLD TO CHANGE.

> *We knew that the spiritual atmosphere was shifting over campuses as we prayed and that principalities and powers were being displaced.... It became clear to me that there are realms of authority only accessed through consistent prayer... (Liebscher, 153).*

TESTIMONY OF A WORLD CHANGER

Ruby was a seventh grader who had a vision God would come and revive her middle school. Early in the year, she started a club where students could come to pray and read the Word. After a few weeks a lot of kids stopped coming, and Ruby found herself contending for Heaven to invade MLK Middle School alone. The whole school year had gone by, and every Thursday Ruby would spend her lunch asking God to change the hearts of students and teachers at her school.

As the school year was coming to a close, Ruby had a dream to hold an outreach that would allow her to tell her peers about Christ. With no budget or help, Ruby saw God answer her desire. A local youth pastor was given $1,000 to specifically use for campus ministry, and Ruby's youth pastor was able to connect the two. Ruby decided to host a talent show and at the end of the talent show have someone share about Jesus. Ruby didn't know what to expect, but one Thursday after school over 230 students *and faculty filled the auditorium. Students showcased their talents, and Christ showcased his love. That afternoon 75 students got saved. After the altar call, the MC wanted to thank the Campus Awakening club for putting on such a great event. The crowd was cheering and joining in the time of gratitude. When asked to stand, the club stood up. Only it was hard to notice, because Ruby was the only one standing.*

RUBY

 **DISCIPLESHIP**

Jesus persistently prayed even though He was the Son of God. He chose to model a life for us of continual connection with His Father in Heaven. Jesus' authority came from His Heavenly identity and ceaseless interaction with God. He said, "Most assuredly, I say to you, the Son can do nothing of Himself, but what He sees the Father do; for whatever He does, the Son also does in like manner" (John 5:19). Jesus could *do* what the Father was *doing* (authority) because He was regularly *seeing* His Father (intimacy). Just as a branch cannot bear fruit apart from having the nourishment of the vine flowing into it, so is constant prayer our life source. If we intend to move in world changing power, we need to first have a persistent prayer life.

What does persistent prayer cultivate in the life of the believer? Is it possible to walk in the authority Jesus had?

_____

_____

Imagine what it would look like to do what God is doing in every situation. Describe some of the things you could accomplish in your world.

_____

_____

After instructing His disciples in the Lord's Prayer, Jesus told them a story about someone persistently asking a neighbor for bread at night. He said, "I say to you, though he will not rise and give to him because he is his friend, yet because of his *persistence* he will rise and give him as many as he needs" (Luke 11:8). Then He went on to tell them to ask and continue to ask, seek and continue to seek, knock and keep knocking (see Luke 11:9-13). As a world changer, Jesus has given you access to unlimited power for you to release on earth. There is more if you ask for more. As you continuously request an increase of Heaven on earth, it will cause your world to become more like Heaven.

It is important to remember that persistent prayer isn't a matter of trying to convince God to answer (Liebscher, 155). When you pray with perseverance, you are praying from a position of dominion because Jesus has raised you up with Himself. You are a son or daughter of God, seated in heavenly places and your right is: "…whatever things you ask in prayer, believing, you will receive" (Matt. 21:22).

The Lord gave you a blank check, signed by Him, and promised all the treasury of Heaven is available to you as you pray. Therefore, when you pray, it is not desperation getting you answers, but believing whose you are and praying tenaciously from a position of rest.

> **WHAT IF...***God's will was fulfilled in your world because you believed and prayed unrelentingly until it manifested?*

What would you pray if you knew *whatever* you petitioned would happen?

_____

_____

How often do you give up or question your authority and identity when you don't see immediate results? In what way does Luke 11:8-9 give you hope?

_____

_____

((•)) PRAYER

Before you start today, remember the primary purpose of prayer is communion and intimacy with God. Spend most of your time today receiving His love, worshiping, and thanking Him for all He has done.

Use this Scripture below to worship God and declare how great He is:

> *Lift up your heads, O gates, and be lifted up, O ancient doors, that*
> *the King of glory may come in!* (Psalms 24:7 NASB)

Jesus, You are the One who opens gates and ancient doors over my world today.

Spend some time praying these Scriptures over your life:

> *I say to you, though he will not rise and give to him because he is*
> *his friend, yet because of his persistence he will rise and give him as*
> *many as he needs* (Luke 11:8).

Jesus, You have called me to persistent prayer.

> *Then He spoke a parable to them, that men always ought to pray*
> *and not lose heart* (Luke 18:1).

Jesus, You will make me the light for nations to receive salvation!

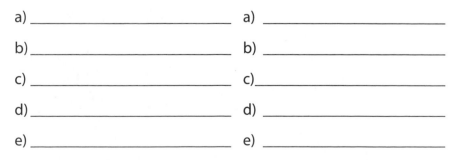 ACTIVATION

Make a list of things you are believing to see transformed, such as sickness, poverty, identity, relationships, systems, and structures. Write these on one side of your page and Heaven's response on the other.

THINGS I WANT TO SEE CHANGED: HEAVEN'S REPLY I WILL PRAY FOR:

a) _____   a) _____

b) _____   b) _____

c) _____   c) _____

d) _____   d) _____

e) _____   e) _____

Now release Heaven's resolution into these situations listed. Commit to praying for these as often as you remember.

YOU ARE CALLED TO CONSISTENTLY PRAY FOR YOUR WORLD TO CHANGE.

FURTHER REFLECTION

Read Matthew 6:9-10. Continue meditating on what it would it look like if your world mirrored Heaven.

TAKING RESPONSIBILITY

WHEN YOU LIVE WITH A SENSE OF RESPONSIBILITY FOR YOUR WORLD, YOU WILL PRAY FOR IT.

Many people don't sustain prayer for their city because they don't feel a sense of responsibility for their region. If you live with a sense of responsibility you will live differently. (Liebscher, 157)

💬 TESTIMONY OF A WORLD CHANGER

Revival has no barriers! At the University of Houston, Jesus has been bringing His Body together in prayer. Recently, the Lord joined ten Christian ministries in 55 hours of continuous praise, worship, and prayer. With hearts focused on a revival from Heaven to transform our campus and nation, we erected a white tent in the middle of campus. The student response was amazing, with over 250 in the night prayer meetings alone! The Lord poured out His Spirit on us as prophetic ministry and salvation flowed out of the tent and spilled onto the campus. This event made the front page of our campus newspaper! We are convinced that as we continue to pour our hearts out to the Lord in unity, He will repeatedly break down religious and denominational barriers—and release revival!

LANCE, campus minister

 **DISCIPLESHIP**

To get nations back on their feet, we must first get down on our knees.
—Billy Graham[1]

When we live with a sense of ownership and responsibility for our city, workplace, or campus, when something happens we don't just roll over and go to sleep, but we rise and do something about it. People sustain prayer for things they feel accountable for.

One of the keys to sustaining prayer is to take personal responsibility for where God has put you. He strategically placed you where you live "for such a time as this" (see Esther 4:14). He planted you as His child and reinstated your original commission to "be fruitful and multiply; fill the earth and subdue it; have dominion…" (Gen. 1:28). God wants you to assume responsibility and use the renewing power He has delegated to you to regenerate the world.

If you live with a sense of responsibility, you will behave differently (Liebscher, 157). In the story of Elisha and the widow, the widow took responsibility for her sons and cried out for Elisha to save them from slavery. It was her determination that activated Elisha into releasing a miracle (see 2 Kings 4:1-7). As world changers we are called to cry to Heaven for those being taken captive around us. We need to say, "Not on my watch!" and use the dominion and authority Christ has given us to set captives free!

On a scale of one to ten, what is the level of responsibility you feel for the sphere of influence where God has placed you? (10 = complete responsibility, 1 = no responsibility) Why?

_____

_____

_____

_____

_____

Ask the Holy Spirit how you could increase this sense of responsibility?

_____

_____

_____

What will you have to change if you take greater responsibility for where God has placed you?

_____

_____

_____

WALKING WITH THE DOVE

Jesus took responsibility to walk continuously in the presence of God. Not only would He regularly withdraw from others to cultivate His Father's presence, but in the midst of life and ministry, He would walk aware of God's presence.

When Jesus was baptized, the Holy Spirit descended on Him like a dove. My pastor, Bill Johnson, uses a profound illustration about the effect a dove on one's shoulder would have. Let's say from this moment on, Jesus walked carefully and humbly so as not to disturb the "dove" on His shoulder (the Holy Spirit). He was fully aware of the Holy Spirit's presence and sensitive to what this "dove" wanted Him to do next.

> **WHAT IF...** *You lived wholly mindful of God's affirmation and words of love for you? How much would this strengthen your life?*

Imagine yourself with Holy Spirit like a dove on your shoulder. What could you do to walk throughout your day with a greater sense of His love and presence?

_____

_____

_____

Spend a few minutes receiving the affection of God and "practicing the presence" of the Holy Spirit. Ask Him to help you sense Him more and ask Him to remind you during the day of His presence.

IS IT POSSIBLE...to learn to walk thoroughly aware of the Holy Spirit and fully responsive to what He purposes to do?

Call a friend and commit to walk entirely attentive to the Holy Spirit's voice, obeying whatever He asks you to do. After today, give your friend feedback on how it went.

_____

_____

_____

((•)) PRAYER

Get alone with God. Welcome the Holy Spirit and thank Him for all that is good in your life.

Use this Scripture below to worship God and declare how great He is:

Let us hold unswervingly to the hope we profess, for he who promised is faithful (Hebrews 10:23 NIV).

Jesus, You have promised and You are faithful.
Spend some time praying these Scriptures over your life:

Then God blessed them, and God said to them, "Be fruitful and multiply; fill the earth and subdue it; have dominion over the fish of the sea, over the birds of the air, and over every living thing that moves on the earth" (Genesis 1:28).

Jesus, You have called me to take dominion.

And the Holy Spirit, in bodily form, descended on him like a dove. And a voice from heaven said, "You are my dearly loved Son, and you bring me great joy" (Luke 3:22 NLT).

Jesus, Your Holy Spirit is upon me and You love me!

ACTIVATION

Ask the Holy Spirit, "Who is on Your heart right now that You want me to pray for?" Allow Him to lead you in prayer. Ask Him for specific people or groups in your campus or workplace that He wants you to intercede for, and follow His guidance in these prayer times.

DEVELOP A SENSE OF RESPONSIBILITY FOR YOUR WORLD...AND PRAY FOR IT.

FURTHER REFLECTION

Read Luke 3:21-22 and 4:1. Ask God what He wishes you to capture from these verses. From this illustration, what does the Holy Spirit bring into the life of the believer?

NOTE

1.   Billy Graham, quoted in "Inspirational Quotes on Prayer," Thoughts About God, accessed March 04, 2012, http://www.thoughts-about-god.com/quotes/quotes-prayer.htm.

DAY 28
BREAKTHROUGH WILL COME

YOU ARE CALLED TO RELEASE BREAKTHROUGH
IN EVERY SITUATION WHEN YOU PRAY!

> *Sustaining prayer isn't so arduous when you believe that God responds to your prayer. You trust breakthrough will come because God answers prayer. Our faith is not in our ability to pray, but in His ability to answer. (Liebscher, 159)*

💬 TESTIMONY OF A WORLD CHANGER

Josh was a popular kid on campus. One night, he went to the prom and then down to the river and drank a lot of alcohol. He passed out, fell down a river embankment, and hit his head on some rocks. His friends thought he'd died, so they left him and ran. The next morning, people found him and took him to the ER. He had alcohol poisoning, and his brain was swollen to the point that nobody thought he'd live, and if he did the doctors expected he would be completely brain dead. Some of the students on campus heard about Josh and said, "He is part of our campus, and we refuse to lose him!" They began to pray. They went to the hospital, and when they couldn't go into the ICU, they prayed over Josh's mom so that she could release healing over Josh. The mom and aunt started crying as the girls ministered to them. Back at school, the principal gave them a classroom to pray in. The group had been praying all year, and he knew they were serious about Josh. Not long after this, they received news Josh was not going to make it. But they didn't give up. They persistently prayed throughout the week. On Wednesday night at youth group, they made a declaration that they were not going to stop praying until Josh was completely well. Suddenly, in the middle of the night, Josh sat up in his hospital bed and spoke. All brain swelling dissipated, and there was no damage from the alcohol or head trauma. None of the predicted residual effects ever developed, and the doctors couldn't believe it to the extent that they kept him for two more days to study why this had happened. Josh showed up to youth group the next Wednesday and told how, "The only reason he was still alive was because of the strangers who prayed for him!" The best part was, after this, Josh got accepted into the military to be a rocket scientist, which he previously did not have the intelligence for. They now rate him a genius!

Praying student

 ## DISCIPLESHIP

Your prayers are potent and effectual to cause a breakthrough in any situation you or others face. Prayer literally moves God, the omnipotent One, and releases Him into action on the earth. Every time you pray in faith, something happens, whether you see it immediately or not. We have a God who is even more eager to show up in our situations than we are desperate. Isaiah says God "acts for those who wait for Him" (see Isa. 64:4). In other words, God is moved to action on behalf of those who seek Him in prayer (Liebscher, 159).

Jesus longs for our prayers to be answered and wants to break through in every situation. He desires it so much, He taught us how to approach prayer: "But when he asks, he must believe and not doubt, because he who doubts is like a wave of the sea, blown and tossed by the wind" (James 1:6 NIV). Our faith is not in our ability to pray, but in His capacity and consistency to answer.

How often is your faith in your prayer rather than God's response? What can you do to shift the focus back on Him?

_____

_____

_____

CHOOSE FAITH

Prayer can happen in two ways—in faith or in doubt. Like two sides of a coin, we choose which attitude we will pray from and reap accordingly.

There is a new breed arising in the earth, electing to pray from faith. Because they flip their attitude from disbelief or uncertainty to trust, they see incredible results! These world changers have bedrock security in the fact their Daddy is all the time good and wants to reveal Himself. They wholeheartedly believe in His faithfulness, so every time they pray, He moves.

Which side of the coin do you usually pray from, doubt or faith? If you find you are skeptical or even ambiguous regarding Heaven's intervention, inquire of the Holy Spirit, "What is the lie I am believing?" Repent and ask Him, "What is the truth?" Record His response and declare it over your life.

_____

_____

_____

_____

REMEMBER TESTIMONIES

One way we can build our convictions is to continually remind ourselves of testimonies of God's steadfastness. Bill Johnson asserts that in Bethel Church's early days, they only had one testimony of healing in six months. So they kept celebrating that testimony and praying for more people until they had another! Today, years later, hundreds of miracles are taking place every week! As a world changer, you are called to steward the accounts of God's allegiance to His Word—and remember His unwavering goodness.

Get alone with the Lord. Welcome Him to speak as you reflect. Make a list of the top five things you are grateful for and spend some time thanking Him for these good things in your life!

_____

_____

_____

_____

_____

If the testimony of Jesus is the spirit of prophecy, what does that mean?

_____

_____

_____

_____

> **WHAT IF...***your testimonies were weapons empowering you to release the same miracles over and over again?*

If testimonies are that powerful, how can you begin to store these treasures and effectively utilize them to extend the Kingdom?

_____

_____

PRAYER

Get alone with God. Welcome the Holy Spirit and thank Him for all the good things in your life.

Use this Scripture below to worship God and declare how great He is:

> *...Then I, God, will burst all confinements and lead them out into the open. They'll follow their King. I will be out in front leading them* (Micah 2:13 MSG).

Jesus, You are the God of the breakthrough.

Spend some time praying these Scriptures over your life:

> But we are not like those who turn away from God to their own destruction. We are the faithful ones, whose souls will be saved. Faith is the confidence that what we hope for will actually happen; it gives us assurance about things we cannot see (Hebrews 10:39–11:1 NLT).

Jesus, You are the God who has given me faith, and with it I can cause the invisible to become visible.

> Beloved, if our heart does not condemn us, we have confidence toward God. And whatever we ask we receive from Him... (1 John 3:21-22).

Jesus, You have given me an answer to *all my prayers*.

 ## ACTIVATION

Think of an issue in your life (or a friend's) where breakthrough is needed. Research two to three testimonies of when God demonstrated His promises for that same area. Pray and declare Heaven's interaction over your situation and believe for breakthrough!

YOU ARE CALLED TO RELEASE BREAKTHROUGH IN
EVERY SITUATION WHEN YOU PRAY.

FURTHER REFLECTION

Read Revelation 19:10. Why do you think it says we worship God when we celebrate the testimonies of Jesus?

DAY 29
JESUS WANTS TO SHOW UP

YOU CAN BE CONFIDENT WHEN YOU PRAY
THAT GOD IS GOING TO SHOW UP!

Can you see it? There's God, on the edge of His seat, excited and eager to be called on…God wants to show up in response to our prayers even more than we want Him to. (Liebscher, 164-165)

💬 TESTIMONY OF A WORLD CHANGER

Living in Northern Thailand, we had put on some extra chunk with the market's Thai-fry, so we decided to exercise more regularly as a family. There's an old airstrip our city has converted to a walking area for the town-folk, so we go out when we can and meet all kinds! It's not the stunning Gold Coast shoreline we are familiar with, but we breathe deep and His presence shows up.

Out striding recently, I came across a beautiful young Thai woman, crouched down crying. Overcome with compassion, I stopped. She shared how she had just got off the phone after hearing her father (a military police officer) was seriously ill in hospital. She allowed my seven-year-old daughter, Armani, and me to pray for her. I spoke peace over her heart and healing for her dad. She smiled, saying she felt much better.

Two days later I saw her again, and she reported that after I prayed, she had called her father and he said, "Don't come to visit me at the hospital now. I'm leaving. I am completely well." Praise God. There is no distance in the spirit!

We are believing this whole family will come to know the Lord and are discovering that as we step out more and more, we are able to rest in the experiential revelation that when we receive and release, He adds!

AJ, writer and activist, 40

DISCIPLESHIP

We serve a great God who delights in giving us the Kingdom! Jesus told a crowd of thousands, "Do not fear, little flock, for it is your Father's good pleasure to give you the kingdom" (Luke 12:32). You can just see His excitement and the joy on His face as you inquire of Him for breakthrough. He will move mountains, part seas, and with the widest smile in the universe, ignite darkness into light! Your Daddy yearns to reciprocate even more than you hope He will answer (Liebscher, 165).

Describe two times the Lord showed up with extravagant goodness!

_____

_____

God finds pleasure in giving the Kingdom to you! Knowing this, how will you pray and what will you pray for?

_____

_____

Jesus demonstrated the goodness of God throughout His life. When the law condemned people, He intervened and forgave them. When sickness crippled people, He was moved by compassion and instructed them to "pick up their mat and walk." When there was any lack or need, those who called on Jesus found Him the most generous Responder in the universe!

But tragically, many people have doubted the goodness of God and reduced Him to a stingy, distant, and cold God. Nothing could be further from the truth. The Bible says, "The Lord is near to all who call upon Him, to all who call upon Him in truth" (Ps. 145:18). God is good to all who beseech Him and are loyal to the *truth* that He is *good*. When we expect and rely on His goodness, He will respond with generosity!

Our persuasion of God's goodness is in direct relation to how well we know Him. The closer we draw to His heart, the more we realize how kind, tender, and unrestrained He is toward us.

What are your expectations of God? How do these affect how He reveals Himself to and through you?

_____

_____

_____

What could you do to receive more of a revelation of the goodness of God?

_____

_____

_____

Spend time imagining the healing of your land. What would it look like? Visualize God's name and His heart entering and overshadowing your world. Outline some miracles you desire to see today and begin to release these in prayer.

_____

_____

_____

_____

How encouraged are you to know God's eyes and ears are open to your confident prayers?

_____

_____

_____

_____

🗼 PRAYER

There is no doubt God will answer our prayers. Jesus said to people who were walking in honor and love with one another that we could, "Ask and it will be given." He didn't say "maybe"; He said it *will* be given!

Spend some time in God's presence. Receive His love and affirmation. Ask Him, "Who do You say I am today?" Write or draw what He tells you.

Praise the Lord and declare these Scriptures over yourself:

> *Do not fear, little flock, for it is your Father's good pleasure to give you the kingdom* (Luke 12:32).

Jesus, it is Your good pleasure to give me the Kingdom today!

> *But you will receive power when the Holy Spirit has come upon you; and you shall be My witnesses both in Jerusalem, and in Judea and Samaria, and even to the remotest part of the earth* (Acts 1:8 NASB).

Jesus, You have given me power to be a witness.

> *Every good gift and every perfect gift is from above, and comes down from the Father of lights, with whom there is no variation or shadow of turning* (James 1:17).

Jesus, You are good and provide good gifts for every need!

 ACTIVATION

Who is someone you can invite into your inner circle who will cause you to grow in your understanding of the goodness of God? Who is someone who can help you burn with greater passion for God? Who is someone who is welcoming and familiar with His Presence? Contact these people today and ask to meet on occasion with them. Lean in to listen and grow from their experience.

_____

_____

YOU CAN BE CONFIDENT THAT WHEN YOU PRAY GOD IS GOING TO SHOW UP!

FURTHER REFLECTION

Read Second Chronicles 7:14 -16.

WHAT IF...humility is simply trusting what God says about you and walking confidently in His righteous identity of you? How would you pray if you were fully aligned to your identity as a son or daughter of God?

DAY 30
SECRETS REVEALED

YOU ARE NOW GOD'S FRIEND AND CAN PARTNER WITH HIM TO SEE HIS DESIRES FULFILLED.

In Christ, God calls us friends with whom He shares His secrets. (Liebscher, 165)

💬 TESTIMONY OF A WORLD CHANGER

Kristina is a junior in high school who has come to know the power of prayer. A few months ago, she converted the closet in her bedroom to her prayer closet. There, she has "secret place" encounters with God to empower her to go public with the ministry of Jesus. She normally gets to school early and walks around the outside gates of the property praying for revival on campus and for God's love to invade her teachers and peers. She knows she is not wasting her time and is on a mission to bring Heaven to earth. Kristina can always be found around campus and even downtown on the streets offering prayer for healing, deliverance, and encounters of God's love. She is never short of a fresh testimony of how the power of God has shown up and done something amazing as a result of her prayer!

Youth pastor, RUSTY GRAVES, for Kristina, student

DISCIPLESHIP

It seems like God's plan was to have us knowing what He was up to. Throughout the Bible, prophets would hear the voice of God for a situation and speak it out, and new circumstances would be created. Today we are under a new and improved covenant in which, as friends of God, we can all prophesy and establish new worlds. Prophecy is truly a key to breakthrough and sustaining God's move in your life.

The new breed of world changers is arising with powerful and accurate prayers because they know what their Father is doing. They have stepped into the reality of friendship and are discovering the fulfillment of working *with* Jesus instead of working *for* Him. They know they are not trying to convince God, but partnering with Him to see His desires fulfilled in the earth (Liebscher, 165). As a friend of God, you have the ability to hear God's dreams and pray them into being.

How much do you feel your prayer life is as a friend of God? Why?

_____

_____

_____

_____

Jesus said, "but I have called you friends, for all things that I heard from My Father I have made known to you" (John 15:15).

When the Lord speaks to us through dreams, prophetic words, biblical promises, and other prophetic experiences, He is providing fuel for our fires of prayer (Liebscher, 159). Any time we become weary in our prayers, the Lord is faithful and sends us a dream or prophetic word or enlivens a Scripture for us. Then the

> **WHAT IF...***friendship with God was something you could begin to progress more into? How would this influence the way you pray?*

strength and courage to continue pressing in ignites our hearts once again. Prophetic revelation is a powerful tool in sustaining faith-filled prayers.

What are some of the prophetic messages God has been saying to you recently? What is the fuel for your fire of intercession?

_____

_____

_____

Beyond learning to *receive* prophetic revelation, we need to develop an understanding of how to *carry* prophetic revelation (Liebscher, 160). This simply means we continually bring our words back to God in prayer. When you receive prophetic words for your life, one of the wisest things to do is write them down and store them. I have pages and pages of prophetic words that have become fuel for my prayer life. I am always revisiting my "words file," reviewing and praying through them as I remind myself and the Lord what He has said. As you build this habit into your life, your prayers will take on a whole new level of meaning. You will be praying, "Your will on earth, as it is in Heaven."

How can you set up a system of recording and organizing your prophetic words so you can revise and pray into them more?

_____

_____

_____

How much more effective do you think it is when we pray with the prophetic messages the Holy Spirit is giving us?

_____

_____

_____

How does it make you feel that God would let you in on His secrets?

_____

_____

_____

What are two of the most distinct prophetic words you've been given? Highlight the key words and main concepts in them.

_____

_____

_____

What can you do to steward these and see them come to fruition?

_____

_____

WHAT IF...you could have fun re-creating the world with God and just enjoy being about His work?

PRAYER

Get alone with the Lord. Make a list of the top five things you are thankful for today and spend some time thanking Him for these good things in your life! Meditate on how amazing He has made you and how generous He is as your friend.

Use this Scripture below to worship God and declare how great He is:

> God is not a man, that he should lie, nor a son of man, that he should change his mind. Does he speak and then not act? Does he promise and not fulfill? (Numbers 23:19 NIV)

God, You speak the truth and then You fulfill it!

Spend some time praying these Scriptures over your life:

> ...But I have called you friends, for all things that I heard from My Father I have made known to you (John 15:15).

Jesus, You have given me the ability to know Your thoughts.

> For I know the thoughts that I think toward you, says the Lord, thoughts of peace and not of evil, to give you a future and a hope (Jeremiah 29:11).

Jesus, Your thoughts are to prosper me and my world.

➡ ACTIVATION

Spend some time looking through the prophetic words you have been given so far over your life. Search for common themes and messages God is highlighting for you to see and believe. Pray into these prophecies and declare who you are. Summarize your words and pin them on your wall to continually see and remember.

_____

_____

**YOU ARE NOW GOD'S FRIEND AND CAN PARTNER
WITH HIM TO SEE HIS DESIRES FULFILLED.**

FURTHER REFLECTION

Read First Kings 18:41-46. Despite the drought, Elijah prophesied rain. How did he participate to see this prophetic word come to full term?

DAY 31
IRRESISTIBLE CRY

YOU ARE GOD'S CHILD AND HE FINDS YOUR CRIES IRRESISTIBLE TO ANSWER!

He will come to us when we call on Him. When we approach Him as children, He turns to us as Father. (Liebscher, 170)

💬 TESTIMONY OF A WORLD CHANGER

Joaquin is a senior in high school. He believes God loves his campus enough to actually go to school with him and change the status quo for His glory. On Mondays, he and his friends have committed to bringing their Bibles and some musical instruments on campus and asking God to open Heaven and come down in His presence. They worship the Lord in the middle of the courtyard during lunch, usually drawing a crowd of passionate revivalists as well as curious onlookers. Joaquin knows Jesus wants to show up, so he simply invites Him as they worship. Students have come to know Christ and the power of His love during these times of worship and intercession. Students have even testified that depression and darkness were lifted off them as they entered in! The ministry of Jesus continues through students like Joaquin, who request Him to come down!

Youth pastor, RUSTY GRAVES,
for high school student, Joaquin

175

DISCIPLESHIP

Just as any devoted father finds it nearly impossible to resist the cries of his son or daughter, our heavenly Father can't help but respond to our cries when we need Him. God is so excited to come when we call because He has adopted us as His sons and daughters. "You received the Spirit of adoption by whom we cry out, "Abba, Father" (Rom. 8:15).

One of the most stunning teachings of Jesus is we can relate to God as a Father in the same way Jesus interacted with Him as a Father. When Jesus instructed His disciples how to pray, He told them to address God, "Our Father in heaven" (Matt. 6:9). In doing so, He was connecting the disciples to God the Father in the same way He was connected to God the Father (Liebscher, 168).

When we call out to Father God, we are demonstrating we belong to Him and His Spirit has taken up residence in us (Liebscher, 170). As Eugene Peterson, author of *The Message* translation, writes:

> This resurrection life you received from God is not a timid, grave-tending life. It's adventurously expectant, greeting God with a childlike, "What's next, Papa?" God's Spirit touches our spirits and confirms who we really are. We know who he is, and we know who we are: Father and children. And we know we are going to get what's coming to us—an unbelievable inheritance! (Romans 8:15-17 MSG)

You have been adopted into the greatest family with the most extravagant Father in the world! You now can approach His throne of grace expecting complete approval and acceptance. As a son or daughter of His House, you are invited to ask, believing you will receive!

What does it mean to you to be adopted as a son or daughter by God Himself?

_____

_____

_____

As an adventurously expectant child, ask God, "What's next Father?" Write down what He says:

_____

_____

Jesus reveals that our heavenly Father is more extravagant than even our best earthly fathers:

> *Or what man is there among you who, if his son asks for bread, will give him a stone? …If you then, being evil, know how to give good gifts to your children, how much more will your Father who is in heaven give good things to those who ask Him!* (Matthew 7:9,11)

Jesus had no question whether the Father would answer Him with good things. We are to have the same attitude because we are sons and daughters of God (Liebscher, 168).

How much greater do you think Father God's love is for us than our earthly father's? How much more does He desire to give to us?

_____

_____

Write some things Father God has promised He would do for us.

WHAT IF...*your Father in Heaven is so happy, generous, and well-resourced that He will do pretty much anything you ask for as His child?*

_____

_____

_____

_____

_____

How does it impact your prayer life to know God will always respond to your cries because you are His child?

_____

_____

If God has positioned you strategically because He wants you to cry out for that area, what are you going to appeal to Him for?

_____

_____

Jesus said, "Ask, and it will be given to you; seek, and you will find; knock, and it will be opened to you" (Matt. 7:7). What are some areas of your world requiring a breakthrough? Write these down, put them on your wall and begin to pray into these until you see Father God break through.

_____

_____

((•)) PRAYER

Get alone with God. Welcome the Holy Spirit and thank Him for all the good things in your life.

Worship Jesus by declaring who He is. Underline parts in these Scriptures that stand out to you and begin to pray them over your life.

Use this Scripture below to worship God and declare how great He is:

> *My salvation and my honor depend on God; he is my mighty rock, my refuge. Trust in him at all times, O people; pour out your hearts to him, for God is our refuge. Selah* (Psalm 62:7-8, NIV).

God, You are gracious and full of compassion to my cry.
Spend some time praying these Scriptures over your life:

> *Or what man is there among you who, if his son asks for bread, will give him a stone? …If you then, being evil, know how to give good gifts to your children, how much more will your Father who is in heaven give good things to those who ask Him!* (Matthew 7:9,11)

Father, You want to give me good gifts when I pray!

> *…So what makes you think God won't step in and work justice for his chosen people, who continue to cry out for help? Won't he stick up for them? I assure you, he will. He will not drag his feet. But how*

much of that kind of persistent faith will the Son of Man find on the earth when he returns? (Luke 18:6-8 MSG)

Jesus, You have chosen me and desire to give me justice and help when I persistently call to You.

ACTIVATION

Think of a friend who is struggling with feelings of being alone and isolated. Inquire of the Holy Spirit for words of affirmation and prophetic words from Father God to them. Write it out, give it to your friend, and pray for him or her.

_____

_____

AS GOD'S CHILD, CRY OUT TO HIM TODAY AND SEE YOUR WORLD CHANGED!

FURTHER REFLECTION

Read James 5:16-18 and Acts 4:31. Think about what stood out to you.

REFLECTION SECTION 4

Get alone with God and spend some time receiving His love and affection for you. Ask Him to speak while you reflect over the previous section.

As you look over the past eight days, how has your vision for prayer grown?

_____

_____

_____

_____

_____

_____

In what way has your view of yourself and God developed? Describe some of the changes in how you see yourself and God, and what this means in the way you now pray.

_____

_____

_____

_____

_____

_____

_____

_____

What are some of the tools or ideas you have learned that you will begin to practice using?

_____

_____

_____

_____

_____

_____

Record some of the miracles and testimonies of what the Lord has been doing in your life over the previous section:

_____

_____

_____

_____

_____

_____

_____

_____

RISKOMETER:

Give yourself a mark on the "Riskometer" scale regarding how you are doing with stepping out and taking risks for God in releasing the Kingdom. (10 = radical risk taker, 1 = not taking any risks.)

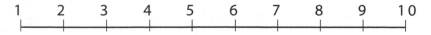

List an area where you will commit to increasing your level of risk taking for God.

Spend five minutes thanking the Lord for all He has done in your life over the last section.

SECTION 5

HEALING REVIVALISTS

DAY 33
LIGHT WINS

YOU ARE CALLED TO SHINE YOUR LIGHT IN YOUR WORLD!

Once you've taken personal responsibility to be the light of the world wherever you are, the next revelation you must have to shine effectively is this: There is no competition between light and darkness. (Liebscher, 181)

TESTIMONY OF A WORLD CHANGER

I recall one afternoon I was in my room and all of a sudden I was thinking about Africa and felt compelled to pray. My heart was so burdened for the continent of Africa to know God. I felt He was giving me words to pray, and I was interceding over and over, "We invite you to come to Africa. We invite you here to Africa. We want you to come…." I felt I was praying on behalf of Africa, and at the time I thought it was strange to be "inviting God" to come, but recognized He was revealing to me His will and how to pray as I partnered with Him. Since then, as I have seen clips on Reinhard Bonnke's ministry (CFAN) in Africa and the millions being saved, I have cried tears of joy for how God is moving there and feel like I am being a part of God's will being fulfilled on the earth. It brings such a sense of purpose, limitlessness, and satisfaction as you participate in what God's doing.

LOUISE, wife, age 29

 DISCIPLESHIP

Light reveals things. The light carried by every believer is the revelation of our King and His Kingdom. Jesus said of Himself, "I am the light of the world" (John 9:5), and then He looked at His disciples and declared, "You are the light of the world" (Matt. 5:14). Jesus never intended your light to stay in private, because His Kingdom (which includes you) is designed to dazzle brightly before others.

Christianity was never designed to be a private party, but a public display of Heaven's good works. Jesus told His disciples, "Let Your light shine before men is such a way that they may see your good works, and glorify your Father who is in Heaven" (Matt. 5:16 NASB).

> **WHAT IF...**_you lived as though your light was more powerful than any darkness around you? Imagine what you could do in your world._

The question then needs to be asked, how do we shine our light? The answer is found in how Jesus shone His light. In John 9, the disciples came across a blind man. Jesus declared His job was to do the will of the One who sent Him because He was the Light of the world. Then He turned to the blind man and healed him. Jesus modeled the fresh standard of what good works are in Christianity. He didn't set up a program to help support the man in his sickness; rather, He shone His light and gave the blind man his sight.

Write down three different stories of when Jesus demonstrated the good works of the Father by shining His Light and destroying the darkness?

_____

_____

_____

When Jesus entered our world, He was establishing a new rule and new rulers on the earth—you and I. He empowered us as "the lights of the world" to completely take over every area of darkness. Wherever there is sickness, we are called to radiate healing. If there is poverty, we shine prosperity. If there is fear and hatred, we emanate love. Jesus made you so powerful as a child of God there is no competition between your illumination and the gloom and obscurity around you. Whenever you turn on your light, the darkness must always leave.

Where in your world are there areas of darkness needing God's light turned on through you?

_____

_____

_____

With your imagination, picture the person of Jesus physically standing in the midst of these situations. Ask Holy Spirit to show you *how* Jesus would shine His light into those specific areas of need. Write what you see Him do in the picture that unfolds. Take a step of faith today and do it!

_____

_____

_____

The enemy is not scared of Christians; he is scared of Christians *who let their light shine* (Liebscher, 184). Jesus' promise to you today is, "…he who believes in Me, the works that I do he will do also; and greater works than these he will do…" (John 14:12).

Right now, the Holy Spirit is inside you, and you have 100 percent of what is required to shine your light, releasing supernatural good works that destroy darkness and despair. It's time to share your light with the public sphere and allow it to shine!

Miracles cause the world to recognize and then give glory to God. Ask Him for a way He is going to use you supernaturally today. Write what you see, hear, and feel.

_____

_____

_____

(((·))) PRAYER

Thank the Lord that He was and is the Light of the World. Thank Him for the miracles He performed in the Bible and ones you have seen or heard of today.

Use this Scripture below to worship God and declare how great He is:

> The Word gave life to everything that was created, and his life brought light to everyone. The light shines in the darkness, and the darkness can never extinguish it (John 1:4-5 NLT).

Jesus, You are the light that can never be extinguished.
Spend some time praying these Scriptures over your life:

> You are the light of the world. A city that is set on a hill cannot be hidden (Matthew 5:14).

Jesus, You have made me the light of the world.

> For we are His workmanship, created in Christ Jesus for good works, which God prepared beforehand that we should walk in them (Ephesians 2:10).

Jesus, You are the God Who prepares good works for me.

ACTIVATION

Go somewhere unconventional and worship God. Maybe it is in a restaurant or on a bench at school. Focus on His love for you. Think on the thought, *"You love me so much, Father."* Keep lifting up the name of the Lord and welcoming His presence until you feel the atmosphere shift. Now focus on the fact that *you* are the light of the world and God has turned on the light in that place. Follow the Holy Spirit's leading and step out in faith to see darkness leave.

_____

_____

_____

_____

YOU ARE CALLED TO SHINE YOUR LIGHT IN YOUR WORLD!

FURTHER REFLECTION

Read Daniel 3. How did God reveal supernaturally that there is no competition between light and dark?

DAY 34
YOU CAN HEAL THE SICK

YOU ARE CALLED TO HEAL THE SICK.

This new breed of revivalists emerging in the earth isn't just going to talk about the Kingdom but will also demonstrate it. They are going to walk in an anointing of power that exhibits to the world around them that Jesus alone has the power to forgive sins. (Liebscher, 205-206)

TESTIMONY OF A WORLD CHANGER

I was in a church in England. My friend had just preached, and I was asked to come onto the stage to prophesy over someone. I noticed a woman in the crowd seemed to be highlighted to me. So I asked her to stand, and I had a word of knowledge that she had a sickness God wanted to heal. She stood there for a moment and then said, "I do suffer from a skin condition called rosacea on my face." I went down to pray for her, but as I did, I felt like God said, "I want the smallest kid in the church to pray for her." So I asked, "Who is the youngest boy in the crowd?" Moments later, a 13-year-old boy came up to me, and I felt God say, "He has a healing gift." The boy was scared, but when he put his hands on her face, they started burning! I could even feel the heat from a foot away! The woman could also sense the heat on her face. The boy asked, "What do I do?" I said, "You are already doing it." After his quick prayer, the woman ran to the bathroom to check her face. When she left, the boy looked up at

me and said, "You don't understand what's happening. I haven't talked
to God for a while. I have just been diagnosed with depression and was
going to kill myself today or tomorrow. I said to God, 'If you get someone
to call me out, I won't kill myself.'" As he shared his story, I began to cry.
My heart was so moved. You see, my father had committed suicide when
I was younger, and it is one of the areas the enemy has to pay me back for.
The boy joined me for the remainder of the time praying for people. The
depression left him, and many others were healed!

ELIZABETH, Bethel intern, age 28

DISCIPLESHIP

John G. Lake taught, "Jesus did not heal the sick in order to coax them to be Christians. He healed because it was His nature to heal."[1] As perfect theology, Jesus modeled Heaven's stance toward sickness. Matthew 9 says, "Then Jesus went about all the cities and villages, teaching in their synagogues, preaching the gospel of the kingdom, and *healing every sickness* and *every disease* among the people" (Matt. 9:35).

Jesus thoroughly represented the Father and Heaven's position on sickness by *healing all*. He saw every hint of affliction as darkness needing to be eliminated. Remember, in Heaven there is no illness, and God's will is, "On earth as it is in Heaven" (Matt. 6:10).

> **WHAT IF...***Christians began to live like Jesus' plan was for health and healing for people?*

If Jesus healed every person who came to Him when He ministered 2,000 years ago, what do you think His position is toward sickness today?

_____

_____

_____

God's Name is Healer (see Exod. 15:26), which means His response to sickness is healing. If He is the Healer and the Bible says He Himself lives inside us, then when we show up, He also shows up—and so does healing.

Jesus never told His disciples to pray for the sick. He told them to heal the sick: "'The Kingdom of Heaven is at hand.' Heal the sick, cleanse the lepers, raise the dead, cast out demons. Freely you have received, freely give" (Matt. 10:7-8).

You have what it takes because God is in you. The Kingdom is within you, and the Lord desires people to be healed even more than you do. Therefore, all the pressure is off you. Ministering healing to someone is not about your ability to pray but *His* intercession for us through the Cross.

Jesus said, "We must work the works of Him who sent Me…" (John 9:4 NASB). Who has God empowered to do the works of healing the sick?

_____

_____

List three people you know who are sick and ask the Holy Spirit to show you how He wants you to pray for them.

_____

_____

_____

((·)) PRAYER

Get alone with God. Welcome the Holy Spirit to come and speak to you as you read. Spend some time thanking Him for all the good things in your life.

Use this Scripture below to worship God and declare how great He is:

…For I am the Lord who heals you (Exodus 15:26).

God, You are the Healer.

Spend time praying these Scriptures over your life:

And as you go, preach, saying, "The kingdom of heaven is at hand." Heal the sick, cleanse the lepers, raise the dead, cast out demons. Freely you have received, freely give (Matthew 10:7-8).

Jesus, You desire to use me to release healing!

And God is able to make all grace abound toward you, that you, always having all sufficiency in all things, may have an abundance for every good work (2 Corinthians 9:8).

Jesus, You are the God Who equips me for every good work!

 ACTIVATION

From this standpoint, thank the Lord for being the Healer of all sickness and disease. Thank Him for investing His miracle power into your life. Take a small piece of paper and ask the Holy Spirit for some clues as to how He is going to move through you today. He may reveal certain conditions, people, or places. Ask Him for divine encounters. While you go about your day, watch and step out to pray for people as you recognize opportunity. Write what happens.

TODAY WALK AS GOD ORDAINED YOU—TO HEAL THE SICK.

FURTHER REFLECTION

Read John 9:1-7. If sympathy talks about the problem but compassion fixes it, what then was Jesus' focus as He encountered the blind man?

NOTE

1.   "Quotes About Healing by John G. Lake," Inspire Ministries, August 24, 2010, accessed March 5, 2012, http://inspireonline.org/quotes-on-healing-by-john-g-lake.

FEAR OVERTURNED

YOU CAN LIVE FEARLESS BY WALKING IN GOD'S LOVE.

The only key I have found to shake off the weight of the fear of people is to remain secure in what the Lord thinks about me. (Liebscher, 188)

TESTIMONY OF A WORLD CHANGER

I was out ministering in the city and I began to ask God whom I should speak with. I saw two men walking through a crowd and was drawn to the smaller man. I felt God say, "The smaller one has a sore toe on his right foot." So I thought, "It's all or nothing. I might as well see what God wants to do." I approached the two men who were now standing in a dark corner of the veranda, like they were about to do a drug deal. I cautiously started a conversation, eventually asking the smaller man if he had a sore right foot. Without blinking, the man responded rudely, "No," as if to say, "leave us alone!" But I wasn't deterred, and began sharing stories of how Jesus was healing people everywhere. Just as I was about to leave, the smaller man spoke up and said, "OK! I do have a sore right toe!" I smiled and asked if I could pray for him. He obliged, and as I prayed, his toe was instantly healed! I spent the next hour playing billiards with the two men and "dealing" the love of God.

EZEKIEL, student, age 24

👥 DISCIPLESHIP

As sons and daughters of God, we are called to live a life that is not controlled by fear and overcome every doubt and dread. The Bible says, "God is love" (1 John 4:8) and "There is no fear in love; but perfect love casts out fear" (1 John 4:18). With God inside you it is not only possible to live without fear's oppression, but you can also assume an offensive position to confront and overcome it.

> **WHAT IF**...*our problem does not flow from the fear of others but a lack of understanding God's love for us?*

Too many Christians conceal their light because they are consumed by the fear of man and suffocated by peer pressure. While we are more concerned with others' opinions than what God thinks, we are robbing the people around us of opportunities to experience the love and power of their Father. When we discern fear, it is important to recognize where it originates. It is not *our* fear, because there is no fear in love. All other fear belongs to another kingdom and its ruler. The truth is, the enemy is afraid of you stepping out because he knows he is powerless. When we move in an act of faith like praying or prophesying over someone, any fear we sense is really not our own but the enemy's, who knows he is about to lose territory. From this perspective, discerning fear should excite you!

When you see an opportunity and sense fear, what should you do before it robs you of releasing God's power?

_____

_____

_____

_____

WHAT IF...it was possible to live fearless of what people thought and to walk in complete boldness, releasing the Kingdom of God in power?

It is possible to transition yourself into a permanent mindset where you are unconcerned about what the crowd thinks. The key in shaking off the weight of the fear of people is to remain plugged in to what the Lord thinks about you. As John wrote, it is when we receive the perfect love of God that all fear is cast out (see 1 John 4:18).

One of the most courageous men in the Bible (King David) tapped into this insight by regularly drawing into his Father's presence to receive His love and His strength. David knew God's thoughts toward him "outnumber[ed] the grains of sand" (Ps. 139:18 NIV), and this imparted an unshakable super-natural courage. God wants to pour so much love into your life you will be unstoppable! As you make time to receive His love each day, social conformity will no longer have a grip because you reach a level of security and confidence through your intimate encounters with Jesus.

How much time do you spend receiving God's love for you? How does this relate to your courage levels in stepping out to shine your light in the world?

_____

_____

_____

God is raising a generation of world changers who know they are radically loved and backed by God Himself. Because of this, they are ready and willing to allow their lights to shine in the public realm where God has placed them. They are so filled with the Father's love; they are not bothered by what anyone else thinks. They approach fear head-on and release the love of God burning inside them.

((•)) PRAYER

Get alone with God. You may want to find a new secret place to be with Him. Welcome the Holy Spirit to come and speak as you read.

Use this Scripture below to worship God and declare how great He is:

The one who does not love does not know God, for God is love (1 John 4:8 NASB).

Jesus, You are the God I know. You are the One who is love.
Spend some time praying these Scriptures over your life:

> *There is no fear in love; but perfect love casts out fear, because fear*
> *involves punishment, and the one who fears is not perfected in love*
> (1 John 4:18 NASB).

Jesus, today all fear leaves me because You love me.

> *Fear not, for I am with you; be not dismayed, for I am your God. I will*
> *strengthen you, yes, I will help you, I will uphold you with My righ-*
> *teous right hand* (Isaiah 41:10).

Jesus, You never leave me and You strengthen me.

ACTIVATION

Write down three things you are afraid of:

1. _____

_____

2. _____

_____

3. _____

_____

Invite the Holy Spirit. "God, You are the God of perfect love. And perfect love casts out all fear. Why am I afraid of each of these things?" Allow the Lord to show you any pictures, thoughts, memories, and so on. He desires to reveal truth and minister to you in His presence.

1. _____

_____

2. _____

_____

3. _____

_____

Ask, "Father, if I give you these things, what will you offer me in return?" (Allow the Lord to show you any pictures, words, thoughts, or promises He wants to show you. Write these down.)

1. _____

_____

2. _____

_____

3. _____

_____

Thank Him for His peace, love and courage. Spend some more time receiving His loving presence before you launch into your day.

Pick one of the fears you listed above and meditate on what He replaced it with. Ask the Lord for a challenge you can do today demonstrating His love has driven fear from your life in that area. Write what He says and step out in love today. Testify what happens below.

_____

_____

_____

LIVE ATTENTIVE TO GOD'S LOVE FOR YOU TODAY,
AND LET ALL FEAR FADE AWAY!

FURTHER REFLECTION
Read First John 4:15-19. What takes place when we abide in God's love? List the outcomes.

DAY 36
DEMONSTRATION

YOU ARE CREATED TO RELEASE THE KINGDOM OF GOD THROUGH SUPERNATURAL POWER.

When John the Baptist became unsure whether Jesus was the Messiah or not, Jesus told John's disciples to go back and tell him what they saw: the blind seeing, the lame walking, and the deaf hearing…. When the world asks us who we are, we should be able to direct them to what we do as evidence of the One we represent.

(Liebscher, 203)

🗨 TESTIMONY OF A WORLD CHANGER

A lady and her son called me over Skype in the Healing Rooms to ask for prayer for healing. She was looking for emotional healing, but I noticed she had glasses on as well as poor hearing. So I prayed for her eyes and her ears, and instantly God restored her sight and opened her ears! Her son then got onto the line and asked if they could also pray for the mother's schizophrenia. So I prayed for the mother again but had no idea if the condition was healed.

A couple of weeks later, I was in the prayer line praying for people at church and a guy came up to me and said, "Hey, you prayed for my mum recently over Skype. She was healed of schizophrenia! For the last 20 years she has suffered, and now she is free!" Then he began to explain how exactly one week from the day of the Skype phone call, all his mother's arthritis left her as well! I didn't realize they had been recording the prayer time on a video camera. He told me he would send me the video of the healing over Facebook! This testimony meant a lot to me personally because sometimes there are certain sicknesses you feel like you have strong faith for and others you don't. When it happened, I had lots of faith for eyes to be healed, but not ears. Now, this particular healing has brought momentum for ears to be healed more often through my life.

ELIZABETH, Bethel intern, age 28

DISCIPLESHIP

Jesus not only talked about the Kingdom, He demonstrated it in power. The Bible says:

God anointed Jesus of Nazareth with the Holy Spirit and with power, who went about doing good and healing all who were oppressed by the devil, for God was with Him (Acts 10:38).

Jesus' strategy for changing the world wasn't to design brilliant programs or create theological debates; instead, He released the power of the Holy Spirit—healing all who were ensnared by the devil. The key to seeing the greatest harvest in the history of the earth is the anointing. If we really want to transform the world, we have to learn to expand the Kingdom of our heavenly Father the way Jesus did. He always spoke the truth in radical love, *backed by demonstrations of power* that validated His authority and revealed who He was (Liebscher, 203).

The apostles and other disciples also took on Jesus' method to see their worlds changed wherever they went. In Acts 3, Peter and John encountered a man born lame. Instead of giving him the currency of earth, they extended the power of Heaven—the ability to walk. Acts 4 records that because of this demonstration of power, 5,000 men made decisions to follow Jesus!

Think of a person everyone knows in your sphere of influence who is in need of a miracle, physically or mentally. What would happen to people's view of God and the Kingdom if you released a miracle into that situation?

_____

_____

_____

_____

How hungry are people for a supernatural encounter with a good God?

_____

_____

_____

_____

In First Corinthians, Paul wrote:

> *And I, brethren, when I came to you, did not come with excellence of speech or of wisdom declaring to you the testimony of God...but in demonstration of the Spirit and of power, that your faith should not be in the wisdom of men but in the power of God* (1 Corinthians 2:1,4-5).

WHAT IF...*we haven't seen our world fully transformed yet because we have been using human manufactured means rather than Holy Spirit power?*

Paul openly demonstrated, "...unusual miracles...even handkerchiefs or aprons were brought from his body to the sick, and the diseases left them and the evil spirits went out of them" (Acts 19:11-12). Just as Paul showed, when we release the Kingdom in power demonstrations, people are immediately awakened to the reality that God is alive and He loves them.

WHAT DO YOU THINK...God is about to do upon our planet as we all begin to step out and release miracles, signs, and wonders?

Across the earth today, sons and daughters are rising up and releasing the power of God into their cities, schools, and workplaces. People are now turning to Him by the thousands, not because of intelligent arguments, but through expressions of a loving God changing their circumstances. Experience always trumps arguments. You are alive for this exciting time and hour to release evidence of the Lord's goodness. As you bring people into experiences with God's kindness, many will be saved and added to the Kingdom because "the goodness of God leads you to repentance" (Rom. 2:4).

Imagine three people in your world who are trapped in negative situations. Dream with the Holy Spirit about what His goodness flowing into these circumstances would look like. Ask Him for an opportunity to release a miracle.

_____

_____

_____

((•)) PRAYER

Get alone with God. Welcome the Holy Spirit to come and speak to you. Spend some time thanking Him for all the good things in your life.

Use this Scripture below to worship God and declare how great He is:

> *Or do you despise the riches of His goodness, forbearance, and long-suffering, not knowing that the goodness of God leads you to repentance?* (Romans 2:4)

Jesus, Your goodness changes hearts!

Spend some time praying these Scriptures over your life:

> *God anointed Jesus of Nazareth with the Holy Spirit and with power, who went about doing good and healing all who were oppressed by the devil, for God was with Him* (Acts 10:38).

Jesus, You have anointed me to a life of power!

Heal the sick, cleanse the lepers, raise the dead, cast out demons.
Freely you have received, freely give (Matthew 10:8).

Jesus, You have given me power to change lives!

ACTIVATION

Spend a few minutes meditating on the verse, "The Kingdom of God is not in word but in power" (1 Cor. 4:20). Imagine your daily routine and the faces of the people you meet. Now visualize breakouts of God's power throughout your day. Write down some of the miracles you see.

_____

_____

_____

_____

_____

Ask the Holy Spirit to help you boldly dispense His power into your world.

YOU ARE CREATED TO RELEASE THE KINGDOM OF GOD THROUGH SUPERNATURAL POWER.

FURTHER REFLECTION

Read Acts 3:1-10 and Acts 4:4. Describe the authority and confidence of Peter and John. How do you think they became so confident to release miracles like this?

DAY 37
RISK TAKERS

YOU ARE CALLED TO RELEASE THE SUPERNATURAL THROUGH TAKING RISKS.

History makers are risk takers, and that radical obedience is the key to supernatural fruit. (Liebscher, 198)

💬 TESTIMONY OF A WORLD CHANGER

This year on the Fourth of July, my brother Greg and I were helping out at a kettle corn concession stand. There wasn't much business, so I suggested Greg and I go and witness on the beach. I said to my bro, "Let's find the largest crowd." We approached a group who were drinking and smoking pot, "Excuse me, everyone. I have come with good news." They shouted back, "We don't want your good news; it's the Fourth of July. We just want to party." Then I started to say, "I didn't come down here to stop you smoking pot and stop you drinking, I came to tell you about the love of God and that He wants to set you free."

As I was preaching, a girl said, "Let's get out of here." Everyone left except one boy. He looked at me and said, "I want what you have got. I want the baptism in the Holy Spirit." I said, "You can pray alone; ask God to save you." He started praying a totally genuine prayer of salvation. He said, "Wow, that was so powerful. I've never prayed before. I knew what to say. What do I do now?" I replied, "You need the baptism in the Holy Spirit." He asked the Lord to fill him with the Holy Spirit. God moved powerfully in his life.

JACOB, Bethel second-year student, age 19

 ## DISCIPLESHIP

History is about to be shaped by the emergence of risk-taking sons and daughters of God. Everywhere these world changers go, they are looking for opportunities to bring people into an encounter with God. They are willing to step out into unknown territory because they believe they can rely on the goodness and love of God. This movement of world changers understands the anointing is released through faith, and as John Wimber noted, "Faith is spelled R-I-S-K."[1]

To truly lead a supernatural life, you need to be willing to take risks in faith.

When Jesus was walking on the water and called out to Peter to come, He wasn't simply inviting His disciple and friend to walk on the water (see Matt. 14:29). Jesus was compelling Peter into the realm He lived in all the time—the realm of the supernatural. And He welcomes us to live there also (Liebscher, 199). Just as He looked at Peter, Jesus has fastened His eyes on you and is entreating you to "come." He is welcoming you to live a supernatural life. Can you hear Him calling?

Take a moment to pause with the Holy Spirit and ask what miracles He is about to do more of, in and through your life.

_____

_____

_____

In order to see these miracles, what are some of the risks (steps of faith) He invites you to take?

_____

_____

_____

We were born to occupy the realm of the supernatural—of healings, the prophetic, angelic encounters, and the gifts of the Spirit. In order to live in the supernatural, we must determine to continually take risks. Too many people are dissatisfied with their Christian walk because they are missing the element of the miraculous in and through their life (Liebscher, 199). However, they remain unwilling to take the plunge into believing God at His Word and trying it out for themselves.

HOW MUCH MORE WOULD YOU GROW...if you subdued the spirit of fear and focused on your spiritual gifts, developing, practicing, and growing in them?

Paul wrote to Timothy:

> *Therefore I remind you to stir up the gift of God which is in you through the laying on of my hands. For God has not given us a spirit of fear, but of power and of love and of a sound mind* (2 Timothy 1:6-7).

WHAT IF...*Jesus wasn't condemning of us when our taking a risk seemed to fail? What if...He was absolutely overjoyed in our willingness to take a risk?*

When he was addressing Timothy, Paul was urging his spiritual son to stir up the heavenly gifts inside and reject the spirit of fear trying to contain him. What gifts was Paul talking about? Spiritual gifts of healing, prophecy, words of knowledge, wisdom, and miracles.

As a son or daughter of God, you are called to exercise the supernatural gifts of the Spirit until they grow into maturity in your life.

Bring to mind a time you have taken a risk and it has seemingly failed. Now remember a time when it has worked out well. Ask the Holy Spirit to reveal what your Father was thinking during these times.

_____

_____

_____

(((•))) PRAYER

Get alone with God. Spend some time thanking Him for all the good things in your life.

Use this Scripture below to worship God and declare how great He is:

> *Heal the sick there, and say to them, "The kingdom of God has come near to you"* (Luke 10:9).

Jesus, Your Kingdom destroys sickness.

Spend some time praying these Scriptures over your life:

> *…But the people who know their God shall be strong, and carry out great exploits* (Daniel 11:32).

Jesus, You allow me to know You and to be strong and do great exploits!

> *For God has not given us a spirit of fear, but of power and of love and of a sound mind* (1 Timothy 1:7).

Jesus, You have given me Your Spirit who is a Spirit of power, love, and a sound mind.

ACTIVATION

In regard to your spiritual gifts of prophecy, healing, words of knowledge, wisdom, etc., what kind of risks have you taken in your walk with the Lord?

_____

_____

_____

Pray and ask God how you can develop further in another area taking risks for the Kingdom. Act on it today and write what happens.

_____

_____

_____

_____

YOU ARE CALLED TO RELEASE THE SUPERNATURAL THROUGH TAKING RISKS.

FURTHER REFLECTION

Read Matthew 14:15-33. How did Jesus teach His disciples?

NOTE

1.   My friend, Christy Wimber, told me that her father-in-law, John Wimber, would say, "Faith is spelled R-I-S-K."

DAY 38
SHAKING OFF FAILURE

YOU OVERCOME FAILURE BY SHAKING IT OFF AND FOCUSING ON WHAT GOD IS DOING.

Bill Johnson told me one time that the difference between men and women of God who go down in the history books and those who don't is the former were not afraid to fail for God. We must progress beyond our fear of failure if we are to be effective in the Kingdom.

(Liebscher, 206)

💬 TESTIMONY OF A WORLD CHANGER

I was hanging out with my friend Phil and we happened to be getting a drink at the 7-Eleven on Mission Avenue in Santa Cruz, California. Beyond snacks, something life changing happened to me that day.

The guy who was working the register had a brace on his wrist, so Phil asked if he could pray for him. He answered Phil in emphatic tones, "No way, bro." The guy was annoyed, in fact. Phil was completely un-phased. We wandered out of the 7-Eleven toward our car, and I was pumped. Something about my friend's lack of fear broke my own.

I saw a guy about ten yards away from where we were standing putting up some kind of poster on a telephone pole, and I immediately sensed in my spirit the Lord telling me to go tell him that He loved him. No second thoughts this time—no wrestling over whether or not I was hearing God. I began walking over to the guy, tapped him on the shoulder, and out came the fateful words, "Hey bro, just wanted to tell you that Jesus loves you man." This was followed by the guy's fateful reply: "You're a freak, man!"

The words flew hard at me but landed like water off a duck's back. I actually felt energized by the rejection. The thing I had been forever afraid of (being thought of as a freak) had finally come upon me, and you know what…it wasn't that bad! No big deal actually. I strolled back over to Phil and he threw it out there, "Way to charge it, bro. That wasn't that bad was it?" I'm like, "Nope, not that bad at all."

Some people would call this whole scenario a "failure" because no one was healed or met Jesus. But I got free that day from the fear of man. Success granted.

LANCE

DISCIPLESHIP

If we truly hope to change the world, then our lifestyle needs to be one of continually stepping into the unknown and taking risks of faith. In order to maintain a lifestyle of boldness, we must always focus on what God is doing and never become entangled by what doesn't appear to be working out.

Sometimes when we step out and take risks, things don't always unfold as planned. The disciples discovered this when they were unable to help a young boy by casting out a demon:

Then one of the crowd answered and said, "Teacher, I brought You my son, who has a mute spirit. And wherever it seizes him, it throws him down; he foams at the mouth, gnashes his teeth, and becomes rigid. So I spoke to Your disciples, that they should cast it out, but they could not" (Mark 9:17-18).

There it was—one huge, in-your-face *failure*. However, although confronted by their inadequacies, the disciples didn't retreat into defeat and abandon their identity and mission. Rather, they shook off the sense of failure and moved forward. After watching Jesus set the boy free, the disciples probed further as to why they hadn't been able to help him. "And when He had come into the house, His disciples asked Him privately, 'Why could we not cast it out?'" (Mark 9:28). They were eager to explore and expand. Therefore, Jesus could divulge more to them, and they became better equipped for the future. Because they moved beyond alleged failure, more people were empowered, more miracles broke out, and the Kingdom of God was extended in a greater way.

Have you ever stepped out and taken a risk to pray for someone but nothing seemed to happen? What did you learn from this? How did you respond?

_____

_____

_____

_____

_____

Many Christians try to step out and take risks, and when things don't work out they become distracted or discouraged and quit trying. But what if God is equally blessed with you taking a *risk* as the *results*? The Bible doesn't say,

> **WHAT IF**...*we viewed the times our risks for God didn't work out as stepping stones to help us learn and grow to the next level of anointing?*

"Without results it is impossible to please God." It says, "Without faith it is impossible to please God" (Heb. 11:6 NIV). The Lord is pleased with us just because He sees us taking risks for His Kingdom. Like an earthly father watching his boy learn to ride a bike, God doesn't love you any less when you fall off. He just wants you to not give up, to remain teachable and keep trying. God wants us to take risks because we are called to greater things. He sees you healing all sicknesses, raising the dead, and casting out demons, and this requires that you step out, practice, and discover.

How can you create a lifestyle of turning aside from failure, shrugging off disappointment, and taking more risks for the Kingdom?

_____

_____

_____

_____

If you wish to learn to walk in the realm of the supernatural, you must face your hesitation and embrace every situation as an opportunity to grow. When you reach out in faith and obedience to pray for someone who is sick or prophesy over a person or situation, then you are a success no matter what happens—so long as you continue to learn from every experience. Risks will eventually pay off, and people with a vision to change the world are ones willing to take risks (Liebscher, 207-209).

PRAYER

Get alone with God. Welcome the Holy Spirit to come and speak to you as you read. Spend some time thanking Him for all the good things in your life.

Use this Scripture below to worship God and declare how great He is:

What then shall we say to these things? If God is for us, who can be against us? (Romans 8:31)

Jesus, You are for me and nothing can stand against me!
Spend some time praying these Scriptures over your life:

But we all, with unveiled face, beholding as in a mirror the glory of the Lord, are being transformed into the same image from glory to glory, just as by the Spirit of the Lord (2 Corinthians 3:18).

Jesus, as I behold You, You are taking me from glory to glory.

Without faith it is impossible to please God... (Hebrews 11:6 NIV).

Jesus, I please you when I step out in faith!

 ACTIVATION

What is an area of the supernatural where you have failed and then pulled back from stepping out and taking risks? Ask the Holy Spirit to show you a vision of yourself five years from now operating in that particular realm of the supernatural. Write it down.

_____

_____

_____

_____

_____

_____

Repent, ask the Holy Spirit for courage, and begin to step out again with His vision in your mind.

SHAKE OFF FAILURE, FOCUS ON WHAT GOD IS DOING, AND KEEP TAKING RISKS TODAY.

FURTHER REFLECTION

Read Luke 10:1-11. What were some risks Jesus asked His new disciples to take? How would you feel about doing this?

DREAM! AND TURN YOUR WORLD UPSIDE DOWN!

YOU ARE CALLED TO A LIFESTYLE THAT TURNS YOUR WORLD UPSIDE DOWN!

> *Something inside of us knows we were not meant to sell "sugared water" for the rest of our lives; we were meant to change the world…. (John Sculley, quoted in Liebscher, 210)*

💬 TESTIMONY OF A WORLD CHANGER

I couldn't believe my eyes. People were living in, of all places…the dump? After this eye-opening trip to Mexico, I knew I was called to be a missionary. I was 19; Jesus was my Treasure and I was thrilled to bring Good News to these people.

Then I learned the bad news about the Good News: So many have never heard it! Tragically, about 135 million people have no access to the knowledge that God loves them and has sent his Son.

But, God is gifting innovators with cutting edge technology to reach the lost. As new tools are forged, passionate hearts brandish these weapons of mass instruction!

Today, my husband David and I visit a remote tribe in the Amazon. David began designing solar projectors and audio Bibles so they can grow in God's Word. (It's difficult to find the Treasure without the "Treasure Map.")

After we showed the Jesus film for the first time, the chief who was on his deathbed was suddenly healed. He began to dance for joy and told everyone, "This Jesus came, not just for the white man, but for our tribe as well!" That small beginning is leading to what will become a great awakening!

STEPHANIE, missionary

DISCIPLESHIP

You and I will never be satisfied to just lead "good" lives; we were destined to make an impact. Our time on earth must change the course of world history. We long to see Jesus exalted in the nations and God's glory covering the earth. This is the call of God on our lives. Jesus Christ has chosen and ordained you to plunder hell and populate Heaven. He has entrusted you with the greatest revival the world has ever seen.

Throughout history, there have been great moves of God that have started then waned, but you are called to perpetuate a revival without end. The prophet Isaiah said:

Of the increase of His government and peace there will be no end. Upon the throne of David and over His kingdom, to order it and establish it with judgment and justice from that time forward, even forever. The zeal of the Lord of hosts will perform this (Isaiah 9:7).

Habakkuk also prophesied, "For the earth will be filled with the knowledge of the glory of the Lord, as the waters cover the sea" (Hab. 2:14). God's plan is not for this new outpouring to explode and then fizzle, but for you to step into His power and increase it until it covers every corner of your world, every family, and every heart.

How will you commit to God's call with every cell of your being?

_____

_____

How will you ensure this revival never ends in your life? What things will you do to ensure your world has an encounter with the knowledge of the glory of the Lord?

_____

_____

_____

Psalms 45:16 says, "Instead of Your fathers shall be Your sons, whom You shall make princes in all the earth." Is there anyone you are investing seeds of revival into who will reproduce the Kingdom in their world?

_____

_____

_____

As a world changer, I want to charge you to live for a generation you will never see. Influence as many people with the Kingdom of God as possible. Teach and build others, displaying the supernatural life and encouraging others to do the same. Dream with God and plan for an

WHAT IF..._you lived for a generation you will never see?_

impact of 100 years from your life. Imagine what God can accomplish through your life. Jesus said:

> The kingdom of heaven is like a mustard seed, which a man took and sowed in his field...when it is grown it is greater...and becomes a tree, so that the birds of the air come and nest in its branches (Matthew 13:31-32).

Do you really aspire to change the world and have the change endure? God has done all He can to make you successful. Now the ball is in your hands. Eternity awaits you. It is your time to dream big!

Kris Vallotton suggests, "If your memories are greater than your dreams, then you're already dying."[1] How do you relate to this statement? Is there anything you need to do to reignite life and hope?

_____

_____

_____

WHAT IF...you left the world better than when you found it by creating and stepping out with your Father?

Just as Jesus cast such an immense vision into His followers that they were willing to give everything to spread the good news of the Kingdom of God, today He stands before you. He commissions you into the same calling, inheritance, and power which caused these simple fishermen to become, "...These who have turned the world upside down" *(Acts 17:6).*

As a son or daughter of God, it is your turn to take the reins of history.

PRAYER

Get alone with God. Welcome the Holy Spirit and thank Him for all the good things in your life.

Use this Scripture below to worship the Lord and declare how great He is:

> *For the earth will be filled with the knowledge of the glory of the Lord, as the waters cover the sea* (Habakkuk 2:14).

Jesus, You will cover the earth with Your Glory!

Spend some time praying these Scriptures over your life:

> *But when they did not find them, they dragged Jason and some brethren to the rulers of the city, crying out, "These who have turned the world upside down have come here too"* (Acts 17:6).

Jesus, You have made me as one who turns the world upside down!

> *You are of God, little children, and have overcome them, because He who is in you is greater than he who is in the world* (1 John 4:4).

Jesus, as Your child I am an overcomer because You are in me!

ACTIVATION

Dream with God...while reading Matthew 13:31-32. Ask Him, "What seed do You want me to plant in the world that will flourish and multiply?"

What things has God called you to accomplish beyond your own ability and possibly extending further than your lifetime/generation?

_____

_____

_____

TAKE HOLD OF YOUR LIFE TODAY, AND WITH GOD, TURN YOUR WORLD UPSIDE DOWN! OR...GIVE THE LORD REIGN TODAY, AND TOGETHER TURN YOUR WORLD UPSIDE DOWN!

FURTHER REFLECTION

Read First John 4. Underline the word *love* in this chapter. How important is love going to be in empowering you to change your world?

NOTE

1.   Kris Vallotton, *Heavy Rain* (Ventura, CA: Regal Ministries, 2010), 184.

REFLECTION SECTION 5

Get alone with God and spend some time receiving His love and affection for you. Ask Him to speak to you as you reflect over the previous seven days.

As you look over the last seven days: What has stood out to you the most regarding your identity and what you are now capable of?

_____

_____

_____

_____

_____

_____

What have been the main two things that you have learned about releasing healing?

_____

_____

_____

_____

_____

_____

_____

How has your view of what God has called you to do grown? Describe some of the changes in how you now see your purpose on the planet.

_____

_____

_____

_____

What are some dreams that you are now going to pursue?

_____

_____

_____

_____

_____

_____

RISKOMETER

Give yourself a mark on the "Riskometer" scale regarding how you are doing with stepping out and taking risks for God in releasing the Kingdom. (10 = radical risk taker, 1 = not taking any risks.)

```
  1     2     3     4     5     6     7     8     9    10
  |-----|-----|-----|-----|-----|-----|-----|-----|-----|
```

List two areas where you will commit to increasing your level of risk taking for God.

Congratulations on completing this training journey! Today is the last day of the book, but the beginning of your lifestyle as a world changer! I want to encourage you to stay connected with world-changing friends, and stay under covering, and together empowered by God, change your world!

APPENDIX A
A WORLD CHANGERS 40-DAY JOURNEY WITH FRIENDS

Below is a suggested timeline for how you could run a 40-day journey with friends. One of the ways to use this book with friends is to set six meeting times throughout the 40 days of the journey (see the table below). During these meeting times, your group can reflect on the good things God is doing and what they are learning and receive any prayer and encouragement for where they are heading. Outside of these six friend get-togethers, there are five sections (of varying length) where the individuals in your group will journey by themselves before you meet the next time. Remember, this is just a suggested timeline. Feel free to modify it to suit the needs of your group of friends.

THE START OF THE JOURNEY Meeting Time:	FRIENDS' MEETING #1 Meeting Place:
Section 1: The New Breed (Days 1-9)	Individual's Journey for 8 days
DAY 9 Meeting Time:	FRIENDS' MEETING #2 Meeting Place:
Section 2: Under Covering (Days 10-15)	Individual's Journey for 5 days
DAY 15 Meeting Time:	FRIENDS' MEETING #3 Meeting Place:

Section 3: The Burning Ones (Days 16-23)	Individual's Journey for 7 days
DAY 24 Meeting Time:	FRIENDS' MEETING #4 Meeting Place:
Section 4: Those Who Pray (Days 24-32)	Individual's Journey for 8 days
DAY 32 Meeting Time:	FRIENDS' MEETING #5 Meeting Place:
Section 5: Healing Revivalists (Days 33-40)	Individual's Journey for 7 days
DAY 40 Meeting Time:	FRIENDS' MEETING #6 Meeting Place:

SUGGESTED FLOW AND LEADER TIPS

In order to get the most out of your time together it's important to have someone who is facilitating and leading your group. Choose a facilitator who will be the one to ask the questions and direct the conversation. Here are five suggestions for things that you as a facilitator could do each time you meet:

1. Welcome and hang out

2. Prayer and share testimonies

3. Group discussion questions

4. Extra challenge (if you have time)

5. Prayer

6. Finish up

Here are a few extra tips for the group facilitator on how to lead a group:

- Have fun!

- Bring your Bible and your copy of the book, Journey of a World Changer.

- Having food is a great way to bring people together and get them relaxed and talking.

- Spend time at the start finding out how everyone is doing.

- Always kick your session off with testimonies of the good things that God is doing. Ask people about the greatest step of faith they have taken that previous week and what they learned about God and themselves from it.

- Make sure everyone gets an opportunity to share. There may be quieter ones in your group and there may be louder ones. To involve quieter people, gently direct questions to them to help them enter discussions, if needed.

- Follow the Holy Spirit. If He is emphasizing something, go with that. Don't worry about getting off the schedule if you need to. You don't want to spend too long on something, but you also don't want to cut something off when the Lord is on it.

- At the end, there are some "Extra Challenges" that you might like to do if you have time.

- Make sure you always have time to pray for each other at the end.

- Text or call your friends throughout the "Individual's Journey" times to encourage them and see how they are doing.

INTRODUCTION: FRIENDS' MEETING #1

The purpose of today's first meeting is to get to know each other, become familiar with the workbook, and pray for one other as you begin your journey into the first section, "The New Breed."

WELCOME AND HANG OUT

Welcome everyone and spend ten minutes hanging out and finding out how everyone is doing.

SHARE AND PRAYER

For the next five minutes, take turns sharing what you would each like to glean from the 40-day journey. Pray for your group as you start today.

GROUP DISCUSSION QUESTIONS

Spend five minutes walking everyone through the work book. Show them the five sections and some of the chapter titles and opening quotes. Ask if there are any topics or testimonies that stand out to them.

Spend 10 minutes working out where you are going to meet over the course of the 40 days and at what times. Fill these into the table provided above.

PRAYER

Spend the last 20 minutes praying for each other. Focus on one person at a time and ask again what they want to gain from the 40-day journey, as well as any specific areas where they need the Lord's help or what they want to grow in. Have each individual ask God for a "picture," Scripture, or word regarding what He is going to do for them over the next 40 days. Reinforce their hope in the fact that the Lord desires greater intimacy and power for them also.

FINISH UP

Spend the last five minutes encouraging everyone about the coming section, "The New Breed," which they are launching into over the next seven days. Make sure all are clear what day, time, and place you will meet next.

THE NEW BREED: FRIENDS' MEETING #2

The purpose of today's meeting is to reflect over the last eight days of journeying through "The New Breed" and to pray for each other as you continue your journeys.

WELCOME AND HANG OUT

Welcome everyone and spend ten minutes hanging out and finding out how everyone is doing.

SHARE AND PRAYER

- It is always very important to focus on what God is doing, not on what He is not doing. Have people share with the group some of the testimonies of what God has been doing in their lives over the previous section.

- Spend the first five minutes praying for your time together and thanking God for His goodness. As we give thanks for every good thing, these testimonies will only increase.

GROUP DISCUSSION QUESTIONS

- As you look over the last eight days, would you say your identity has grown? Outline how your view of yourself has developed and what this means for your future.

- How has your perspective of the Lord grown? Describe some of the changes in how you now see God and what this means in how you relate to Him.

- How has your sense of purpose and vision grown? Explain how this has developed and in what way it is practically influencing your daily routine.

- Share with the group a recent step of faith or risk that you took.

EXTRA CHALLENGE

As a group, spend some time downloading words of knowledge for each other. Form two lines, and stand back-to-back with your friends. Have one line of people close their eyes. Have a person mix the people up in the other line so no one knows who is behind them. Now instruct the line of people with their eyes closed to ask the Holy Spirit for the birth month or favorite color of the person standing behind them. Give them one minute before asking them to share. Encourage them God is happy with their risks, and the more they practice, the more accurate they will become.

PRAYER

Spend 15 minutes praying for and encouraging one another with words from God.

FINISH

Remind your group that your next meeting will be in six days. Plan and write down in the table above where and when you will meet next. As people leave, encourage them to keep stepping out of their comfort zones and taking more risks.

UNDER COVERING: FRIENDS' MEETING #3

The purpose of today's meeting is to reflect on the previous five days of journeying, "Under Covering," and pray for one another as you continue your journeys.

WELCOME AND HANG OUT

Welcome everyone and spend time hanging out and finding out how everyone is doing.

SHARE AND PRAYER

- Have people share with the group some of the testimonies of what God has been doing in their lives over the previous section.

- If there are certain testimonies that are highlighted to you, ask if anyone in your group needs a breakthrough in that area. "The testimony of Jesus is the spirit of prophecy" (Rev. 19:10). Pray for those people who respond to the invitation and release God's power to do it again in their lives.

GROUP DISCUSSION QUESTIONS

- As you look over the last five days, how has your understanding grown in regard to the importance of spiritual covering?

- How has your view of spiritual covering changed or grown?

- Who would you say is your spiritual covering? Share how you maintain strong connections with your fathers and mothers. Be as transparent as you can regarding how you have received discipline and correction and in what way this has helped you in the long run.

- What are the two practical things that God has highlighted to you that you will take from this section and put into practice in your life?

- Describe some of the changes in how you now see God's vision for the generations working together.

- What are two things you are excited about God doing in and through you and your spiritual covering in the near future?

- Share with the group a recent step of faith or risk that you took.

EXTRA CHALLENGE

In groups of three, make up a card, poster, or some other creative way to prophesy and bless your church leader, youth pastor, or parents. Bless them radically and thank them for everything they are doing for the Kingdom.

PRAYER

Spend 15 minutes praying for and encouraging each other with words from God.

FINISH

Remind your group that your next meeting will be in eight days. Plan and write down in the table above where and when you will meet next. As people leave, encourage them to keep stepping out of their comfort zones and taking more risks.

THE BURNING ONES: FRIENDS' MEETING #4

The purpose of today's meeting is to reflect on the previous seven days of journeying, "The Burning Ones," and pray for each other as you continue your journeys.

WELCOME AND HANG OUT

Welcome everyone and spend time hanging out and finding out how everyone is doing.

SHARE AND PRAYER

- Have people share with the group some of the testimonies of what God has been doing in their lives over the previous section.

- Again, if there are certain testimonies that are highlighted to you, ask if anyone in your group needs a breakthrough in that area. "The testimony of Jesus is the spirit of prophecy" (Rev. 19:10). Pray for those people who respond to the invitation and release God's power to do it again in their lives.

GROUP DISCUSSION QUESTIONS

- As you look over the last seven days, what has been a common theme the Holy Spirit has highlighted for you to learn and grow in?

- In what ways have you developed in your understanding of God's love for you? How has this affected you?

- How passionate are you for God and what things do you find trying to take away your passion for Him?

- Share how you have decided to say yes to Jesus during the busyness and options of your day.

- How do you handle the times when you make wrong choices and don't choose Jesus? How do you continue walking in His acceptance and love?

- What are the top three things you are going to do to be still and receive God's love this week?

EXTRA CHALLENGE

As a group, get together and spend 15 minutes soaking in the love of God and worshiping Him. Your goal is to fill yourselves up with a tangible awareness of His passion for you. Share with each other about what you are experiencing. If you want to take it further, why not take the love of God out onto the streets?

PRAYER

Spend five minutes thanking God for all He has done in your life over the last section.

FINISH

Remind your group that your next meeting will be in nine days. In the table above, plan and write down when and where you will meet. As people leave, encourage them to keep stepping out of their comfort zones and taking more risks.

THOSE WHO PRAY: FRIENDS' MEETING #5

The purpose of today's meeting is to reflect on the last eight days of journeying, "Those Who Pray," and pray for each other as you continue your journeys into the fifth and final section.

WELCOME AND HANG OUT

Welcome everyone and spend time hanging out and finding out how everyone is doing.

SHARE AND PRAYER

- Have people share with the group some of the testimonies of what God has been doing in their lives over the previous section.

- Again, if there are certain testimonies that are highlighted to you, ask if anyone in your group needs a breakthrough in that area. "The testimony of Jesus is the spirit of prophecy"

(Rev. 19:10). Pray for those people who respond to the invitation and release God's power to do it again in their lives.

GROUP DISCUSSION QUESTIONS

- As you look over the last eight days, how has your vision for prayer grown?

- What does your time with God generally look like? How much of your time with God is about intimacy with Him?

- Where is your secret place? Share one of your greatest encounters with God and how it has changed you.

- How has your view of yourself and God matured? Describe some of the changes in how you now see yourself and the Lord, and what this means in how you pray.

- What are some areas that you are persisting in your prayer life for breakthrough?

EXTRA CHALLENGE

In your group ask the Holy Spirit, "Who is on Your heart right now that You want us to pray for?" Allow Him to lead your group in prayer. Ask Him for specific people groups around the nations, specific issues, key leaders, etc., that He wants you to intercede for, and follow His lead in these prayer times.

PRAYER

Ask your group, "What is the biggest breakthrough that you want to see happen in your life?" Spend time as a group praying and prophesying over each other and release breakthrough into these areas.

FINISH

Remind your group that your next meeting will be in eight days. Plan and write down where and when you will meet. As people leave, encourage them to keep stepping out of their comfort zones and taking more risks.

HEALING REVIVALISTS: FRIENDS' MEETING #6

The purpose of today is to reflect on the last section, "Healing Revivalists," and pray for each other as you finish up the workbook and continue your journeys to change your worlds.

WELCOME AND HANG OUT

Welcome everyone and spend time hanging out and finding out how everyone is doing.

SHARE AND PRAYER

- Have people share with the group some of the testimonies of what God has been doing in their lives over the previous section.

- Again, if there are certain testimonies that are highlighted to you, ask if anyone in your group needs a breakthrough in that area. "The testimony of Jesus is the spirit of prophecy" (Rev. 19:10). Pray for those people who respond to the invitation and release God's power to do it again in their lives.

GROUP DISCUSSION QUESTIONS

- As you look over the last seven days, what is the most prominent truth you have learned regarding your identity and what you are now capable of?

- What have been the main two things you learned about releasing healing?

- How do you handle disappointment, for example, when prayers don't seem to be answered straight away? What were some of the keys from the book?

- What are some miracles or healings that you would like to see God do through your life? How could you step out more to see these happen?

- How has your view of what God has called you to do grown? Describe some of the changes in how you now see your purpose on the planet.

- What are some dreams you are now going to pursue?

EXTRA CHALLENGE

In groups of two or three, go somewhere in your city and begin practicing words of knowledge. Ask the Holy Spirit for some details of people who are sick. Begin asking around if anyone has those conditions, and ask if you can pray for them. Release healing into peoples' lives!

PRAYER

- As a group, read Isaiah 60:1-3 and Isaiah 61:1-4 over yourselves as a declaration of who you are and what you are now going to do.

- Spend 20 minutes praying for each other and encouraging each other with words about your futures.

FINISH

Today is the last day of the book, but the beginning of your lifestyle as a world changer! As a group, decide if you would like to meet up regularly to share testimonies of what God is doing and to continue to encourage each other as you change your world.

Congratulations on completing the 40-day journey with your friends! The best is yet to come! Keep stepping out, keep trusting in Jesus, and keep changing your world!

APPENDIX B
CONFESSIONS

LETTING GOD NAME YOU

When we wake in the morning we can declare over ourselves who God says we are. When we speak this out and believe it, we are agreeing with Him and creating new worlds with our words. Here are some declarations to get you started:

HE RECEIVES ME AS HIS OWN

- I am a royal son of God. (See John 1:12.)

- I have been made perfect and I have peace with God. (See Romans 5:1.)

- I am united with God, and I am one with Him in spirit. (See First Corinthians 6:17.)

- I am free from all condemnation. (See Romans 8:1-2.)

I AM SECURE AND CONFIDENT

- God has plans for me, to prosper me, to give me a future and a hope. (See Jeremiah 29:11.)

- If God is for me, then who can be against me? (See Romans 8:31.)

- God works all things out for my good. (See Romans 8:28.)

- I am a minister of reconciliation for God. (See Second Corinthians 5:17-21.)

I AM DESTINED FOR GREATNESS

- I can do all things through Christ who strengthens me. (See Philippians 4:13.)

- God is making the world better, and I am co-laboring with Him today. (See Isaiah 9:7.)

- I am God's masterpiece, re-created in Christ to do good works which He has planned long ago. (See Ephesians 2:10.)

- I have the mind of Christ. I receive world-changing ideas from God. (See First Corinthians 2:16.)

ABOUT BANNING LIEBSCHER

BANNING and SEAJAY LIEBSCHER have been on staff at Bethel Church in Redding, California for over 10 years. They are the directors of Jesus Culture, a ministry dedicated to mobilizing, equipping, activating, and sending a new breed of revivalists all over the world. These revivalists are encountering God, burning with passion for Jesus, being trained and equipped in the realm of the supernatural, and being sent into their cities to minister in power. Prior to his current position, Banning was the youth pastor at Bethel Church and a lead overseer in the School of Supernatural Ministry.

In the right hands, This Book will Change Lives!

Most of the people who need this message will not be looking for this book. To change their lives, you need to put a copy of this book in their hands.

> But others (seeds) fell into good ground, and brought forth fruit, some a hundred-fold, some sixty-fold, some thirty-fold (Matthew 13:8).

Our ministry is constantly seeking methods to find the good ground, the people who need this anointed message to change their lives. Will you help us reach these people?

> Remember this—a farmer who plants only a few seeds will get a small crop. But the one who plants generously will get a generous crop (2 Corinthians 9:6).

EXTEND THIS MINISTRY BY SOWING
3 BOOKS, 5 BOOKS, 10 BOOKS, **OR MORE TODAY,**
AND BECOME A LIFE CHANGER!

Thank you,

Don Nori Sr., Founder
Destiny Image
Since 1982

DESTINY IMAGE PUBLISHERS, INC.

"Promoting Inspired Lives."

VISIT OUR NEW SITE HOME AT
WWW.DESTINYIMAGE.COM

FREE SUBSCRIPTION TO DI NEWSLETTER

Receive free unpublished articles by top DI authors, exclusive
discounts, and free downloads from our best and newest books.
Visit www.destinyimage.com to subscribe.

Write to: Destiny Image
                   P.O. Box 310
                   Shippensburg, PA 17257-0310

Call: 1-800-722-6774

Email: orders@destinyimage.com

For a complete list of our titles or to place an order
online, visit www.destinyimage.com.